THE USBORNE

PLAYING CHESS

Susan Caldwell
Illustrated by Dee McLean
Additional illustrations by Sarah McCaig
Designed by Sharon Martin
Series Editor: Lisa Watts

SCHOLASTIC INC.
New York Toronto London Auckland Sydney

Contents

ISBN 0-590-48006-5

12 11 10 9 8 7 6 5 4 3 2 1 4 5 6 7 8 9/9

Printed in the U.S.A. 23

First Scholastic printing, March 1994

How to use this book

This book is a basic guide to chess for absolute beginners. With colorful step-by-step pictures and instructions, it clearly and simply explains the rules of the game and how to play.

The different moves of each of the chess pieces are clearly shown in the pictures with bright green arrows. A red arrow shows that a piece is being attacked and a red circle shows it has been captured.

Once you have mastered the basic rules and how the pieces move, picture-by-picture instructions take you through the different stages of the game and advise on the best moves to make. It is a good idea to follow the moves on your own chess board as you read this book.

On most of the pages there are chess puzzles for you to do to test your skill and help you recognize the best moves to make. The answers to the puzzles are at the end of the book.

The best way to improve your chess is to play lots of games. You can play with other people, or you can follow the games printed in chess books, magazines and newspapers. For this you need to be able to read notation – the shorthand way of writing down chess moves – explained on pages 21 and 59.

If you come across a chess word you do not understand, in this or other chess books, you can look up the meaning in the list of words on page 64. Then, if you want to know more about it, you can turn to the page number given in brackets next to the word.

Starting off

Chess is a game for two people. Each person has an "army" of sixteen pieces, and the object of the game is to trap your opponent's King.

The pieces

At the beginning of the game the pieces are set up on the board as shown on the right. One person uses the light-colored pieces and the other plays with the dark-colored pieces. The colors are always called "White" and "Black," even if, as in this book, they are cream and red.

Each of the pieces has to move in a certain way, as shown on pages 6–11. The players take it in turns to move their pieces, and can move only one piece in each turn. Once you have touched a piece, you must move it, and after you have moved it and taken your hand away, you must leave the piece where it is.

The board

Rows of squares across the board are called "ranks" and the rows up and down the board are called "files". Lines of squares running diagonally are called "diagonals".

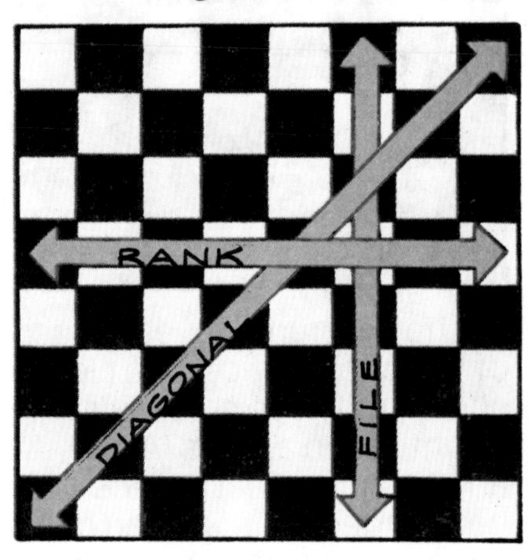

When you set up the board, make sure you have a white square on your right-hand side, and that the White Queen is on a white square and the Black Queen is on a black square.

PAWNS

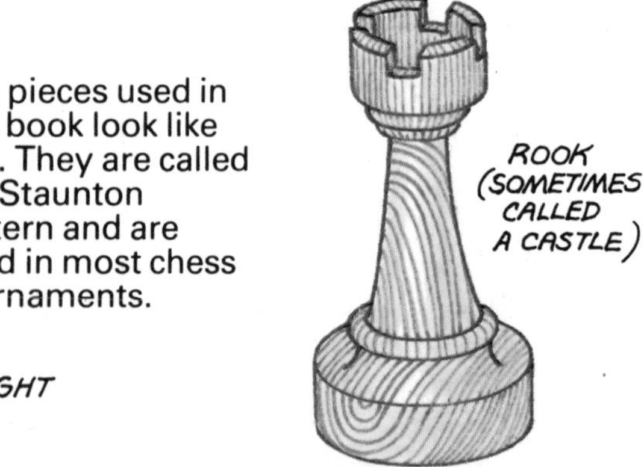

The pieces used in this book look like this. They are called the Staunton pattern and are used in most chess tournaments.

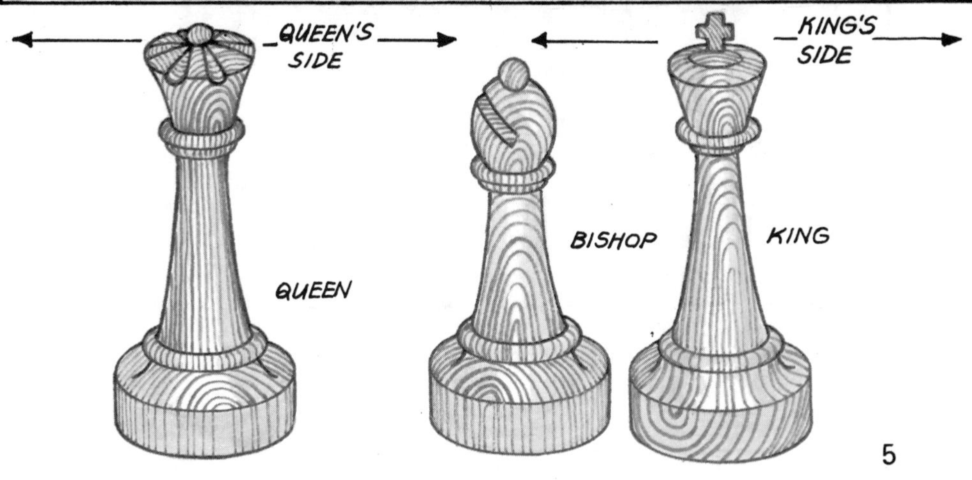
QUEEN'S
SIDE
KING'S
SIDE
BISHOP
KING
QUEEN

The Bishop

Each player has two Bishops. The one that starts next to the King is called the King's Bishop and the one that starts next to the Queen is the Queen's Bishop.

Bishops move diagonally across the board in any direction. They can move any number of spaces in each turn, but they cannot jump over other pieces.

This picture shows how the Bishop can move.

Can the White Bishop capture any of the pieces on this board?*

If there is a piece of its own color in the way, the Bishop has to stop and can go no further along that diagonal.

If there is an enemy piece in the way, like the Knight shown here, the Bishop can capture it.

 **Answer page 60*

The Knight

Each player has two Knights: a King's Knight and a Queen's Knight. The Knight is the only chess piece which can jump over other pieces. It can jump over pieces of its own color, or over enemy pieces.

The Knight can move in any direction, forwards, backwards or to either side, but it always has to move three squares at a time.

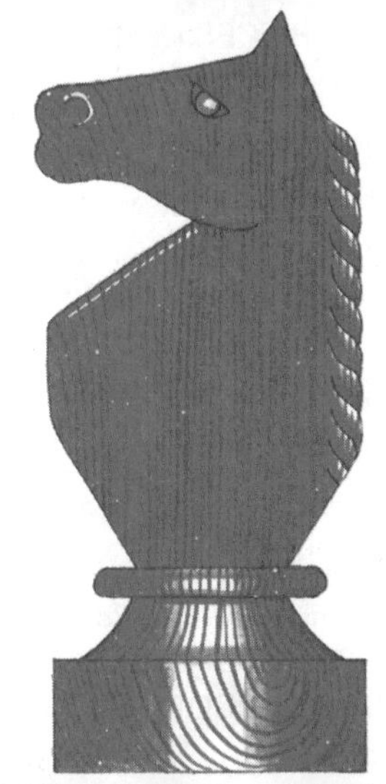

Whenever the Knight moves it must go two squares in one direction and then one square to the side, as shown above.

It can make this move in any direction, as shown here.

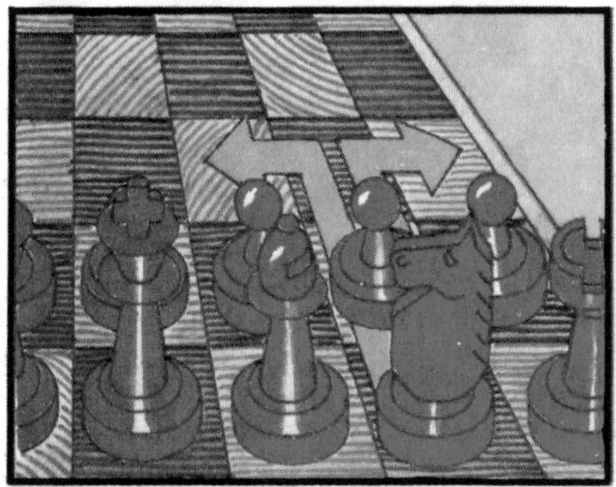

Since the Knight can jump over other pieces, it can move at the beginning of the game before the pawns in front of it move.

If the Knight lands on the square of an enemy piece, that piece is captured and removed from the board.

The Rook

This piece is sometimes called a Castle but Rook is its proper name. Each player has two Rooks and they start in the corners of the board. The Rook can move backwards or forwards, or to either side. It must always move across the board (that is, along the ranks) or up and down the board (along the files). It can only move in one direction in one turn, and cannot jump over pieces.

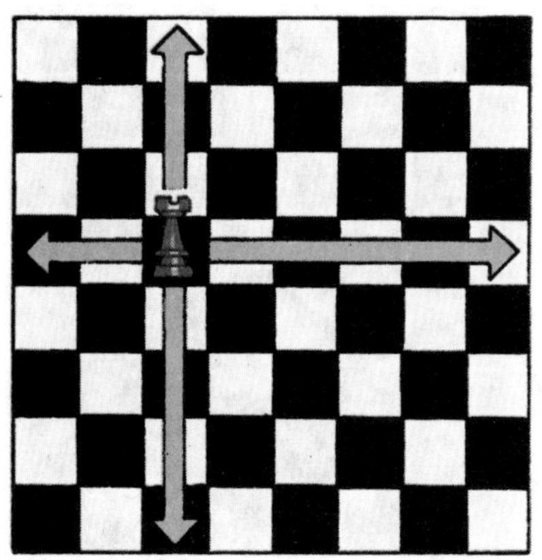

This is how the Rook can move.

The Rook in this picture can land on the same square as the Knight or the Bishop and capture either of them. It cannot take both in the same move.

Can the White Rooks in these two pictures capture any pieces? Be careful not to put them where they can be captured.*

 *Answer page 60

The Queen

The Queen is a very powerful and valuable piece as it can move in any direction. It can move only one way each turn, though, and cannot jump over other pieces.

Each side has one Queen. At the beginning of the game, check that Black's Queen is on a Black square and White's Queen is on a White square. Look after the Queen and be very careful moving it, as it is a very useful piece.

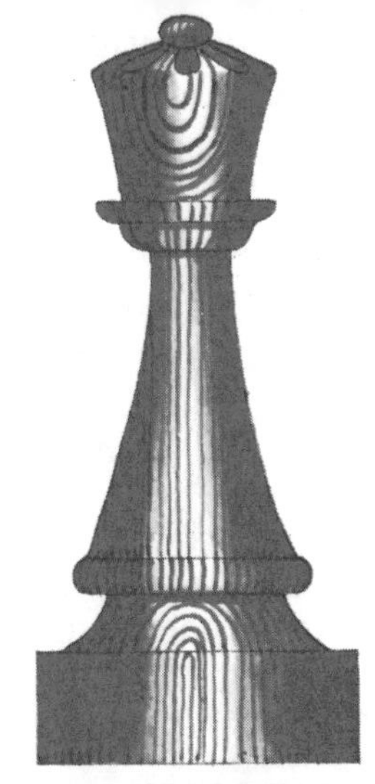

The Queen can move any number of squares in each turn.

Queen puzzle

Which pieces can each Queen capture?*

*Answer page 60

Another Queen

This is the Queen from another chess set, called the "Reynard the Fox" set. The pieces represent the animals from an old folktale. The Queen is a lioness, the King, a lion and the Bishop is a fox.

Pawns

The word Pawn comes from a Latin word meaning "foot-soldier". Each player has eight Pawns, and although they are the least valuable of the pieces, they are very useful.

If one of your Pawns reaches the other end of the board without being captured, you can change it for a Queen, or any other piece except for a King. This is called "Queening" a Pawn.

How Pawns move

Pawns can only move forwards. They can go two squares on their first move, and only one square on every other move.

To capture another piece, the Pawn moves one square diagonally forwards. It cannot take a piece directly in front of it.

If there is a piece in front of it, the pawn is stuck until that piece moves – unless it can move diagonally to capture.

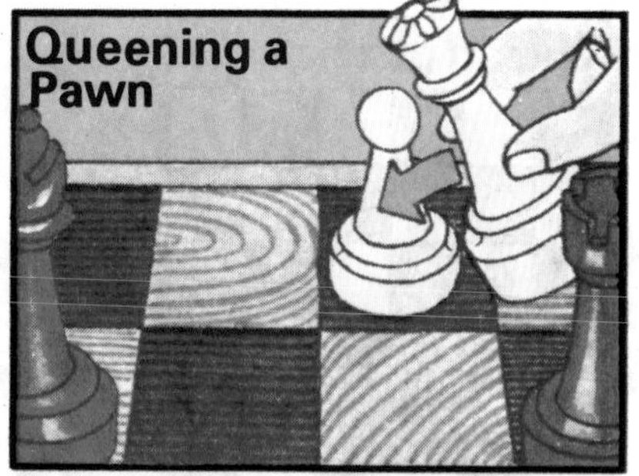

If a Pawn reaches the other end of the board you can make it a Queen. If you still have your Queen, use an upside-down Rook.

The King

The King is the most important piece in the game. You must move it very carefully, for if an enemy piece is placed so that it can capture your King, and the King cannot escape, you lose the game. You should guard the King carefully all the time, and if it is under attack from the other side, move quickly to save it. Watch out, too for opportunities to attack your opponent's King.

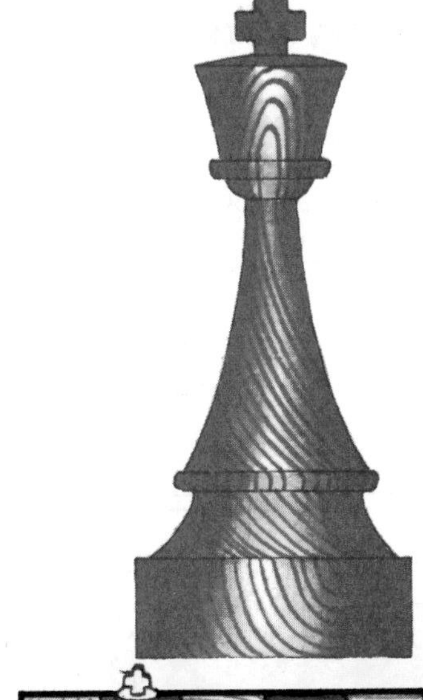

How the King moves

The King can move and capture pieces in any direction, but it can move only one square in each turn.

If the King is in a position where it can be captured it is said to be in "check". The piece attacking it is called the "checking piece".

How to save the King

If your King is in check, you must save it on your next turn. It is against the rules to leave the King in check. There are three ways you may be able to save it:

1. Move the King out of way.
2. Move another piece in front of the King so it is out of the firing line.
3. Capture the checking piece.

You can see these three moves on the right.

Here the Black King is in check from the White Rook.

How to win

The aim of the game of chess is to trap the enemy King so it cannot escape being captured. That is, there are no squares for it to escape to, no pieces to protect it and no piece to capture the checking piece. When this happens it is called "checkmate" and the player with the checking piece, or pieces, wins.

Checkmate

In this picture the Black King is in checkmate from the White Queen, helped by the White Bishop. Since the King can only move one square at a time, it cannot escape to any square out of the Queen's reach. No piece can be placed between the Queen and the King either. The King cannot capture the Queen as then it would be in check from the Bishop, so White wins the game.

Spot the checkmate

On the board below, can you find a move for White to play that checkmates Black? The answer is explained at the bottom of the page.

Answer

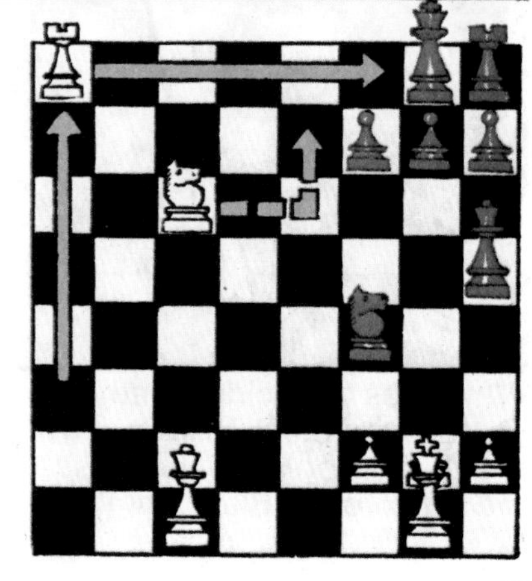

To checkmate the Black King, move the White Rook to the back rank, as shown on the right. Black cannot capture the Rook and has no pieces to put between the Rook and the King. The King can move one square towards the White Rook, but it would still be in check.

If you move the Knight instead of the Rook it would be check, but not checkmate. The King could escape by moving one square to the left.

Capturing pieces

To put yourself in a strong position to checkmate the enemy King, try and capture as many enemy pieces as possible. Sometimes you may have to lose a piece in the battle to capture an enemy piece. You should only do this if it is a fair exchange, that is, if your piece is of the same, or less value, than the enemy piece. To work this out, the pieces are given points, as shown below.

When you capture an enemy piece, you take that piece off the board and put your own piece in its place.

Values of the pieces

The Queen is worth the most points as it is the most useful and powerful piece. The King has no points as it is the end of the game if it is captured.

It is a fair exchange to lose a piece of the same point value as your opponent's piece. So you can lose a Rook for a Rook, or a Bishop for a Knight.

Example

White has to decide whether to capture the Black Bishop with the White Rook and then lose the Rook to the Black Knight.

This is not a good exchange as Black loses a piece worth three points, and White loses a piece worth five points.

Capturing puzzles

Above, should the White Bishop capture the Black Rook?*

Which piece should the Black Queen take?*

Which piece should the White Knight capture?*

* *Answer page 60*

Story of Chess

Chess is a very old game. It is thought to have developed from an Indian game called Chaturanga which was played in India about 1,500 years ago.

Over the centuries, travellers and invaders carried the game across the Middle East and Europe. The rules changed gradually, and it became the game we know today. Now the rules are internationally agreed.

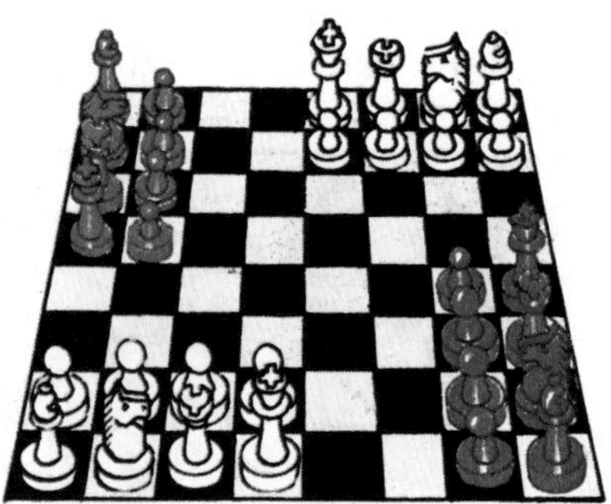

The Chaturanga board was probably set up like this, and the rules were different from those of modern chess. It was played by four people and they used dice to decide how the pieces moved.

Attacking and defending

In this picture the White Rook is moving to a position from which it can attack the Black Bishop.

To save the Bishop, Black can move it to a safe square out of the Rook's line of attack.

Another way is to move the Knight to defend the Bishop. If the Rook captures the Bishop, the Knight can take the Rook.

You should only defend a piece in this way if your opponent is going to lose a more valuable piece than yourself.

Hints

Look carefully before you attack. The square you move to may be guarded. Above, can the Knight safely attack the Rook?*

Try and position your pieces so they defend each other. Which of the pieces under attack from the Queen is not defended?*

 *Answer page 61

Puzzles

Which White piece can attack the Black Rook?*

Which White piece can attack the Black Knight?*

Can Black move a piece to defend the Rook?*

*Answer page 61

More pieces

These chess pieces are thought to be about a thousand years old. They are part of the Lewis set which was found on the Isle of Lewis, off Scotland.

The pieces are made of ivory carved from walrus tusks and are thought to have been brought to the Isle of Lewis by the Vikings.

Castling

This is a special move for the King and the Rook. It helps to keep the King safe in the early part of the game, and brings the Rook to the center of the board where it is in a good position to attack.

Castling is the only time when the King can move two squares, and it is the only time that the Rook jumps over a piece.

To castle on the King's side, move the King two squares towards the King's Rook and jump the Rook over the King.

To castle on the Queen's side, move the King two squares towards the Queen's Rook, then jump the Rook over the King.

Special castling rules

1. It must be the King's and the Rook's first move of the game.

2. There must be no pieces between the King and the Rook.

3. You cannot castle if the King is in check.

4. You cannot castle if the King will be in check in the new position, or if the King passes over a square where it would be in check.

On which sides (the King's side or the Queen's side) can Black and White castle in these two pictures?*

 **Answers page 61*

A special move for Pawns

When a Pawn moves two squares forward on its first move, an enemy Pawn can capture it as though it had moved only one square. This is called *en passant* (pronounced "on passon") which is French for "in passing".

If the Black Pawn shown above moves two squares on its first go, the White Pawn can capture it. White can only do this on his next turn.

Puzzles

In which of these pictures can the Black Pawn capture *en passant* if the White Pawn moves two squares forward?*

Checkmate puzzles

On each of these boards, can you find a move for White that is checkmate?*

**Answers page 61*

Drawn games

Sometimes it is not possible for either side to checkmate their opponent and the game ends in a draw. One kind of draw happens when one of the players can make no legal moves, but is not in check. This is called "stalemate". The other kind of draw is when one player continually puts the other in check. If the same position is repeated three times, the game ends in a draw. This is called "perpetual check". A game may also end with one player resigning and two players may agree to draw if they think neither side can win.

Here, it is Black's turn but if he moves he will be in check from the White King or Queen. The King is not allowed to move into check.

The King is not in check now though, so it is not checkmate and, providing Black has no other pieces to move, the game ends in a draw.

Perpetual check

On this board, the White King is in check from the Black Queen. The White King has to move out of check, to the square shown by the green arrow.

Black can now move the Queen diagonally to the left and put the King in check again. The King has to move back and the Queen can put it in check again.

How to write down chess moves

The code for writing down chess moves is called notation. There are two main systems of notation: algebraic and descriptive. In this book, moves are written in algebraic notation which is explained on this page. Descriptive notation is explained on page 59. Once you can read notation, it is useful to practice games written in books or magazines on your own chess set.

Algebraic notation

SQUARE f5

8 7 6 5 4 3 2 1

a b c d e f g h

Ranks are numbered from White's end. Files are lettered from White's left. Each square is called by the letter and number of the rank and file it is in.

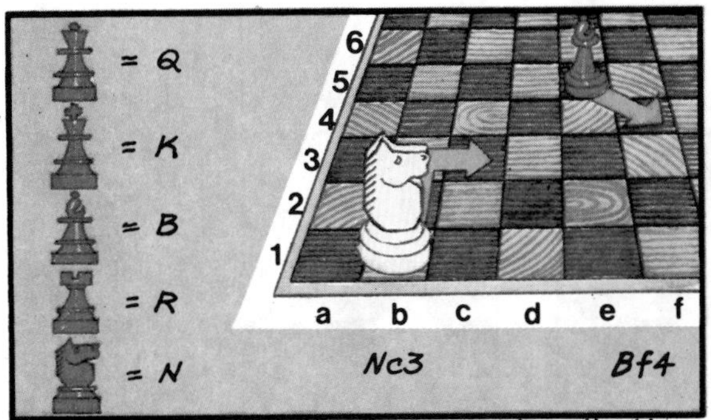

Each piece, except for the Pawn, is called by a letter. To write a move you give the letter of the piece, then the letter and number of the square it moves to.* White's moves are always given first.

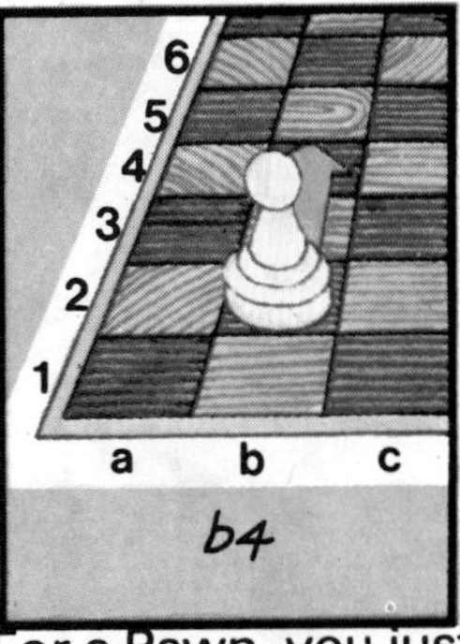

For a Pawn, you just write the letter and number of the square it moves to.

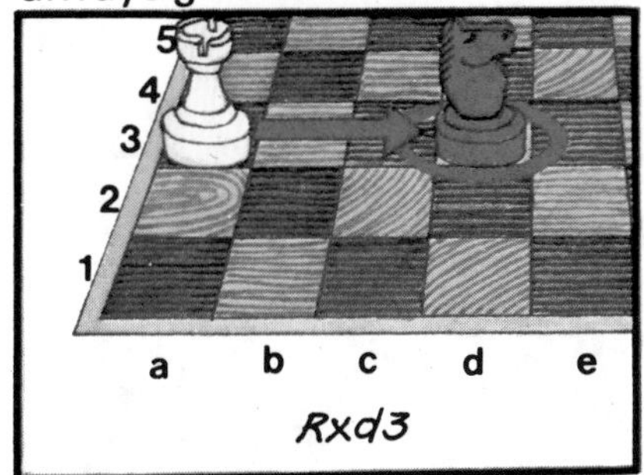

When a piece captures, you write "x" between the name of the piece and the move it makes. Check is written as "+".

Castling on the King's side is written 0-0, and on the Queen's side, 0-0-0.

Put a piece of paper with the letters and the numbers on it under the board to help you find the squares.

A simple game to follow

A good way to learn and to improve your chess is to read games printed in books, magazines and newspapers, and follow the moves on your chess set.

On these two pages there is a short game for you to follow. Each of the moves is given in algebraic notation, with White's moves always given first. Study each of the moves carefully, and try them on your chess board.

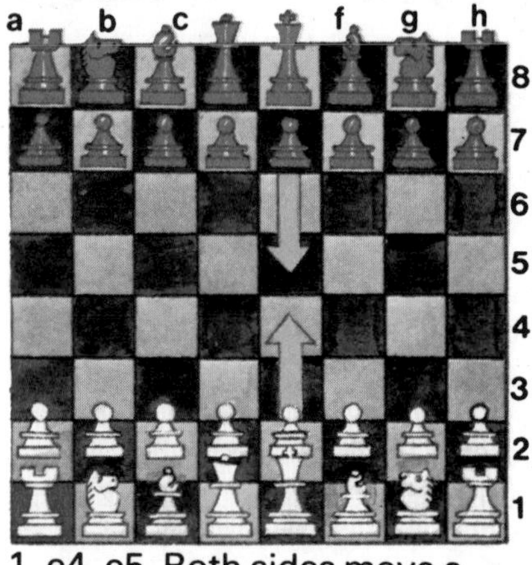

1. e4, e5. Both sides move a Pawn two squares to the centre.

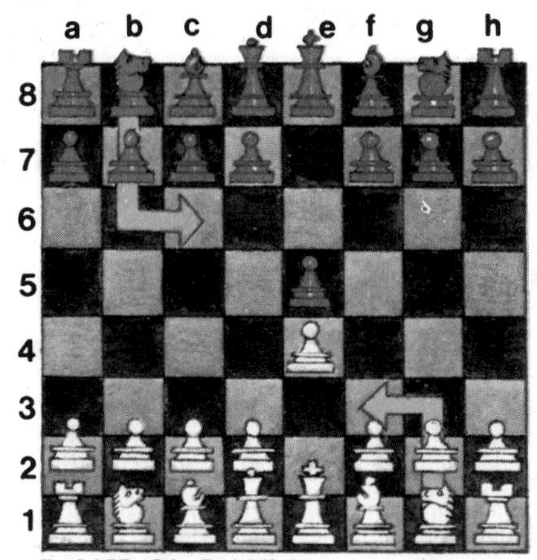

2. Nf3, Nc6. White attacks the Black Pawn. Black defends it.

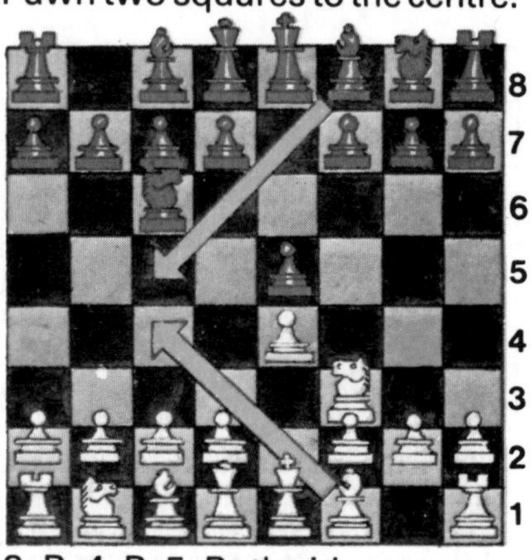

3. Bc4, Bc5. Both sides move a Bishop.

4. 0-0, Nf6. White castles to move the King to a safer place. Black's knight attacks White's Pawn.

5. d3, 0-0. White defends the Pawn. Black castles.

6. Bg5, d6. White moves the other Bishop. Black moves a Pawn to open the way for its other Bishop.

7. Nh4, Qd7. Black should have moved the Bishop as planned.

8. Bxf6, g7xf6. White captures the Knight and the Black Pawn recaptures the Bishop. Both lose a piece of equal value.

9. Nf5, Re8. White moves the Knight, preparing for an attack on the King. Black moves the Rook to a more open file.

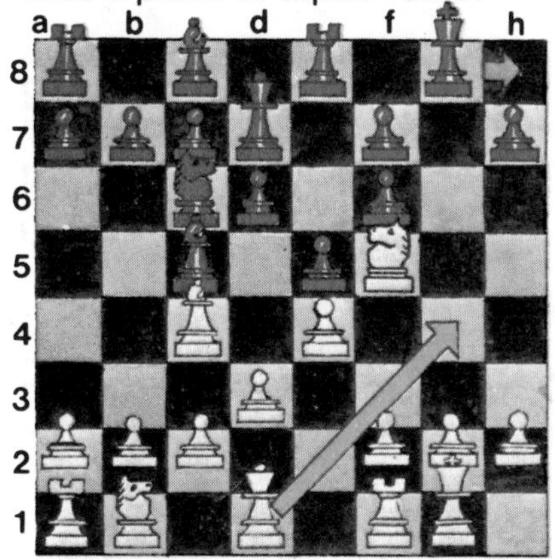

10. Qg4 check, Kh8. The King moves out of check.

11. Qg7 checkmate. The Black King is in checkmate. It cannot capture the Queen as the Queen is defended by the Knight.

How to start a game

The first few moves you make at the beginning of the game are very important. This is your chance to position your pieces in the best way for the struggle in the middle of the game. To start, set up the board as shown on pages 4–5. White always moves first.

The most important thing at the beginning of the game is to move pieces to the center of the board where they are more powerful than near the sides. This is called developing.

Why pieces in the center are powerful

At the edge of the board Bishops can move to only seven different squares, and Knights to only four.

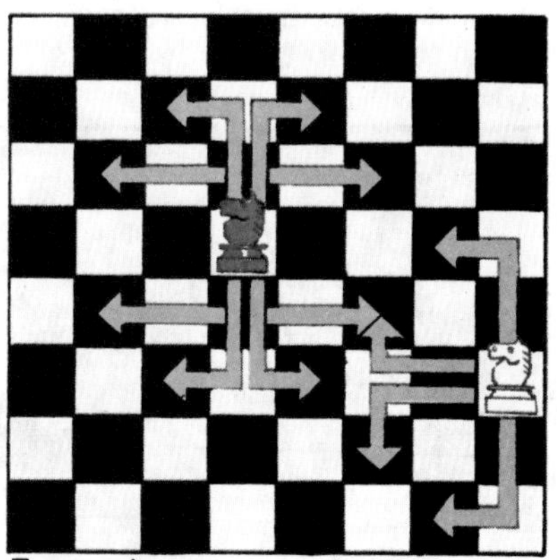

From the centre, the Bishop has a choice of 13 squares and the Knight of eight so they are almost twice as powerful.

Well placed pieces

Here, White's pieces are well developed, with Bishops and Knights near the center where they are most powerful. The Pawns are well grouped together and castling has put the King safely to the side of the board. White's moves followed the rules set out opposite.

First moves

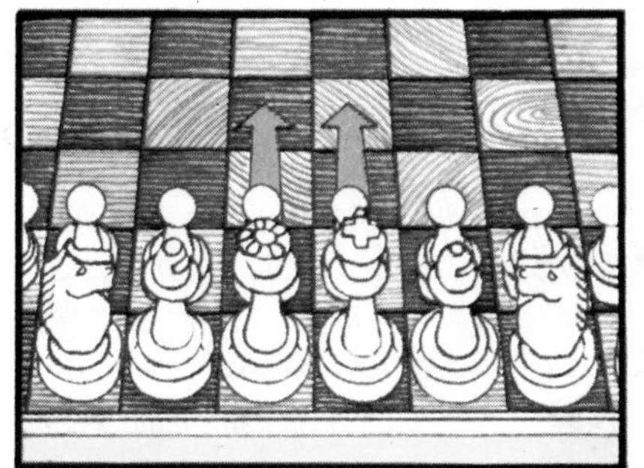

A good first move for both sides is to move one of the center Pawns two squares. This opens the way for the Bishops.

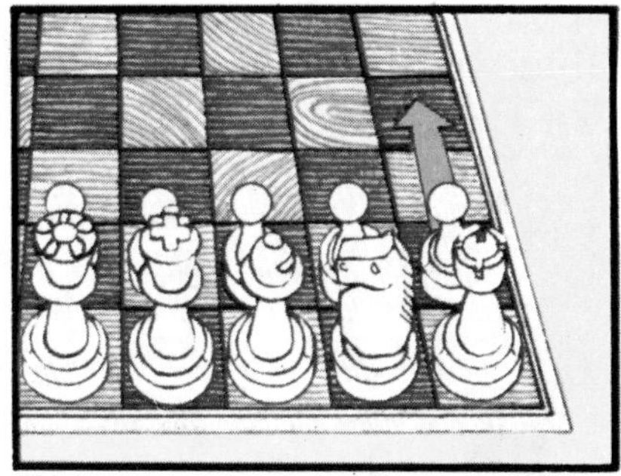

This is not a good move as it does not help control the center of the board. Nor does it open the way for a Bishop.

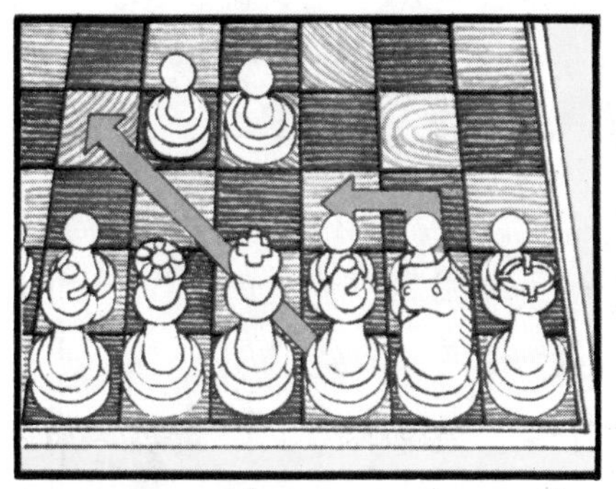

In your next few turns, move the Knights and Bishops out to good central positions. The Knights can defend your Pawns.

Now your back rank is clear for you to castle. Castling keeps the King safe behind protective Pawns at the side of the board.

Puzzles

You have to prepare your pieces for castling (look back to castling rules page 18). Can the White King castle here?*

If your opponent has a piece in the center, you may be able to force it away. How can Black make the White Knight move?*

**Answer page 62*

More about first moves

Try not to waste any of your turns by moving the same piece too often or putting pieces on the wrong squares. Do not bring the Queen out too early, either, or your opponent may chase it around the board.

The board below shows Black's and White's pieces after seven moves. Black's pieces are well arranged, but White has wasted a lot of moves and the pieces are badly placed. The pictures on the opposite page show these first seven moves.

White's position

White has brought out only the Queen and the Bishop, and has only one Pawn in the centre of the board. The rest of the White pieces are still sitting uselessly in the back ranks.

Black's position

Both of Black's Knights and Bishops are very well placed and the King is ready to castle on either side. Black also has two Pawns on centre squares.

How the pieces moved

Both sides put a Pawn in the center, then White moved out a Bishop and Black developed a Knight.

White moved the Bishop back a square — a bad move as it was well placed. Black moved his Bishop to a good center square.

White moved the Queen to attack the Black Pawn and threaten the King. Black could easily defend the King though, then attack the White Queen.

White's Pawn move was bad — it did not help the center. Black developed a Knight which attacked White's Queen.

White had to move the Queen. Black put a Pawn in the center and this opened the way for his Bishop to attack the Queen again.

White moved the Queen out of the Bishop's attack. Black moved the Bishop out and attacked the Queen again.

The danger of being greedy

You may be tempted to capture an undefended Pawn early in the game. Be careful, though, it is not worth neglecting the development of your pieces just for a Pawn.

Always have a reason for each Pawn you move. They should be used to strengthen your position in the center, to defend your pieces and to attack enemy pieces.

The board below shows the positions after seven moves. Black has captured a White Pawn, but the Black pieces are not well placed. You can follow the moves on the opposite page.

White's position

White's pieces are very well placed. Although one Pawn has been captured, White will shortly be able to attack Black's undefended King.

Black's position

Black now has one more Pawn than White, but he has developed only the Queen. The Bishops and Knights are still in their starting positions.

The moves

Both sides put a Pawn in the center. Then White developed a Knight which attacked Black's Pawn.

Black defended the Pawn with another Pawn. This also opened for the Bishop. For the third move, White brought out a Bishop.

Black moved another Pawn, but should have brought out a piece. White's Pawn move defended his pieces and opened for the Bishop.

Black made a bad Pawn move which did nothing to help the pieces in the center. White brought the other Bishop out to a good center square.

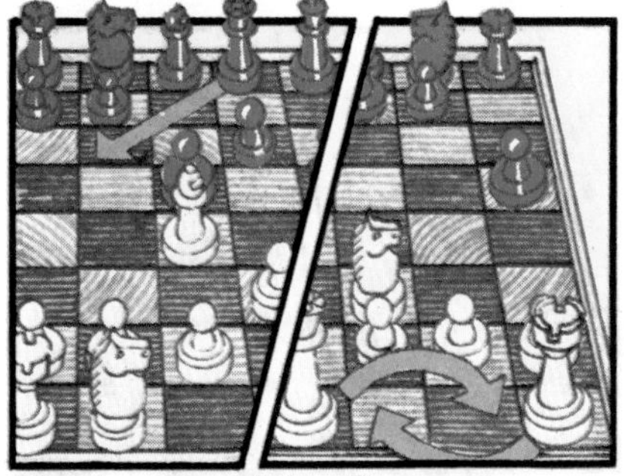

Black moved the Queen to attack White's undefended Pawn, but should have developed a piece such as a Knight. White castled.

Black captured the Pawn and White brought out his second Knight. This gave the positions shown on the big board on the left.

Keeping the King safe

The game on these two pages shows how important it is to castle early to hide your King in the corner behind a row of Pawns. Black loses quickly because the King is left in the middle of the board with no defenses.

Each of the moves is written in algebraic notation (see page 21). The vertical files are lettered a – h from White's left and the ranks are numbered 1 – 8 from White's end.

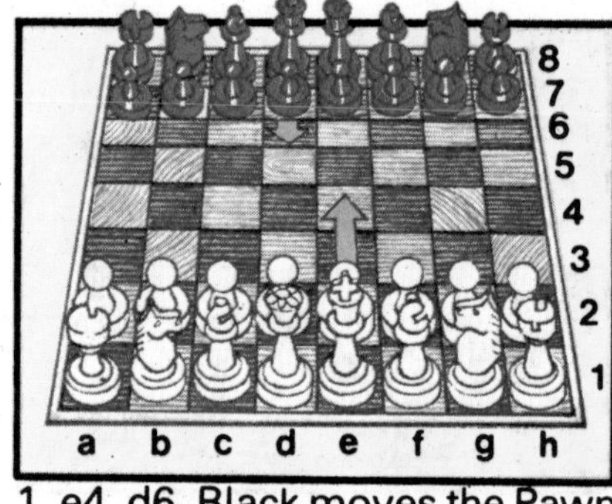

1. e4, d6. Black moves the Pawn only one square. This is alright as it still controls square e5 and opens for the Bishop.

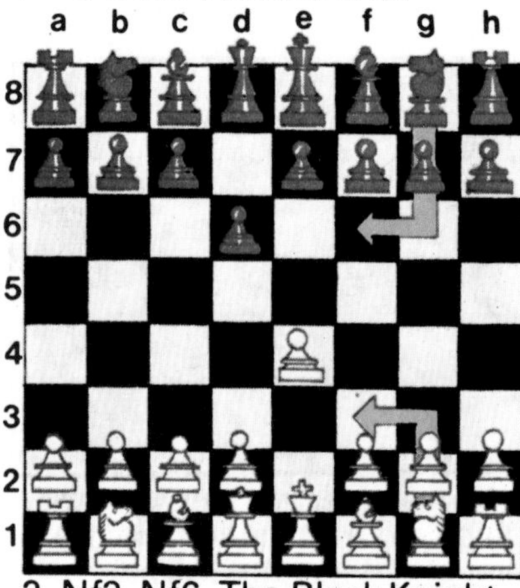

2. Nf3, Nf6. The Black Knight attacks the White Pawn.

3. Nc3, Nc6. White develops a Knight and defends the Pawn at the same time. Black brings out another Knight.

4. Bc4, b6. White moves a Bishop to the center and Black moves a Pawn, planning to move the Bishop to b7 next move.

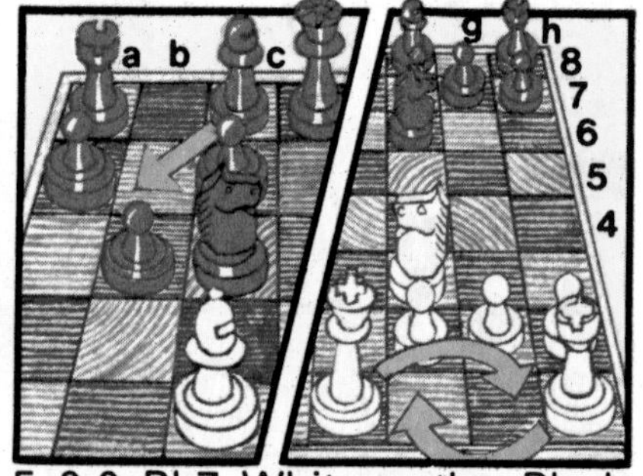

5. 0-0, Bb7. White castles. Black moves the Bishop, but it would have been better to open the other side and castle.

6. d4, e5. Both sides move another Pawn. Black's move is bad though, as you will see from the next move.

7. dxe5, dxe5. White captures Black's Pawn and Black retakes the White Pawn. This is a fair exchange, but it leaves the file open and unguarded.

8. Ng5, Qxd1. The White Knight moves up to attack Black's King's side. The Black Queen captures the White Queen.

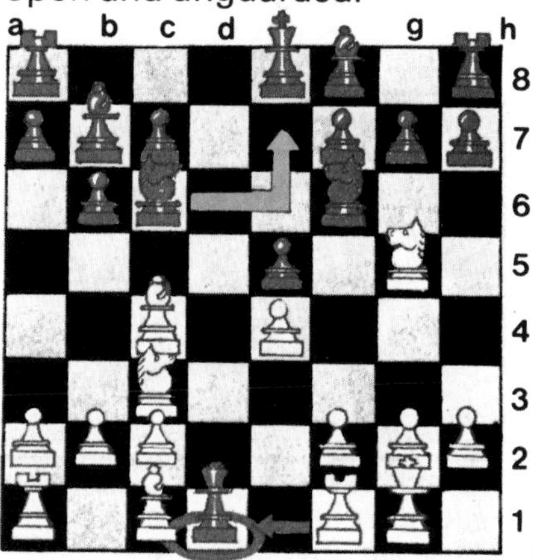

9. Rxd1, Ne7. How could White checkmate next turn?*

Things to remember at the beginning of the game

Move your center Pawns first. Use them to control the center squares, to defend your pieces and attack your opponent. Make sure you have a reason for each Pawn move.

Bring your Bishops and Knights out early in the game. Moving the Queen too soon can waste time, and the Rooks work best on a clearer board later in the game.

Look after your King from the very beginning of the game and castle early to defend it.

*Answer page 62

Ideas for first moves

On the next few pages there are some sequences of moves that Black and White can make in the early part of the game. Some of these moves are named after the tournaments or chess players who made them famous.

It is very good practice to try out the moves, and the various replies you can make to your opponent's moves. If you prefer, though, turn to page 38 and find out about the next part of the game first.

First moves for White

A good first three moves are Pawn to e4, Knight to f3 and Pawn to d4. You may have to adjust these moves though, depending on what Black does.

Sicilian defense

If Black plays 1 . . . c5*, still play Knight to f3 and Pawn to d4. Black will probably take the Pawn with 3 . . . cxd4.

You can then recapture with 4. Nxd4, then go on to develop your pieces and castle.

Alekhine's defense

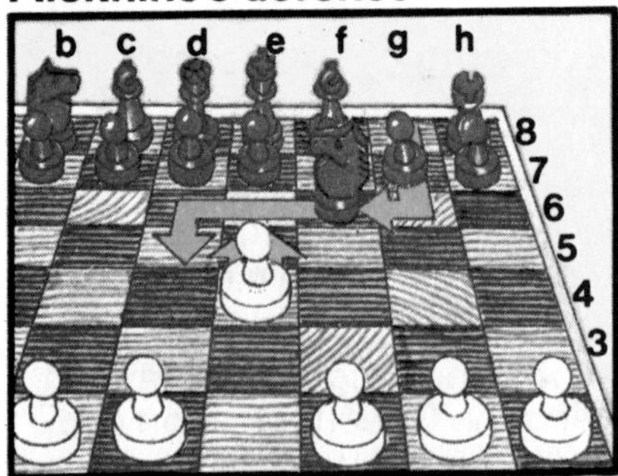

If Black plays 1 . . . Nf6 and attacks your Pawn, you cannot play Nf3 on your second move. Instead move the Pawn to e5 to attack Black. Black plays 2...Nd5.

On your third turn, put a Pawn on d4 to defend the other Pawn. Black will probably move a Pawn to d6 and you can then bring out your Knight to f3.

**When Black's moves are written separately from White's, there are dots between the number and the move.*

First moves for Black

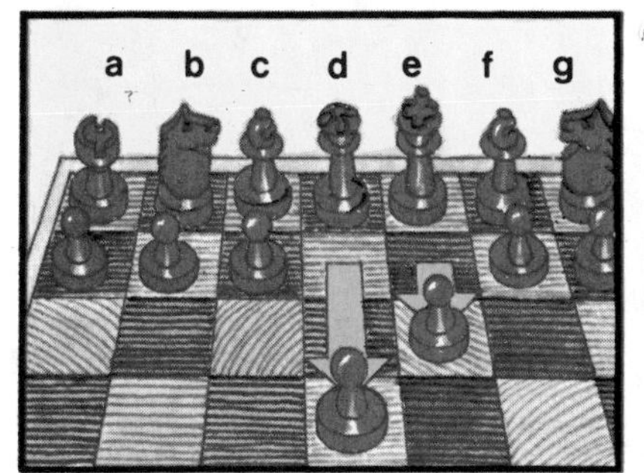

Whenever possible, if you are playing Black, try to play your center Pawns to e6 and d5, then develop your other pieces.

French defence

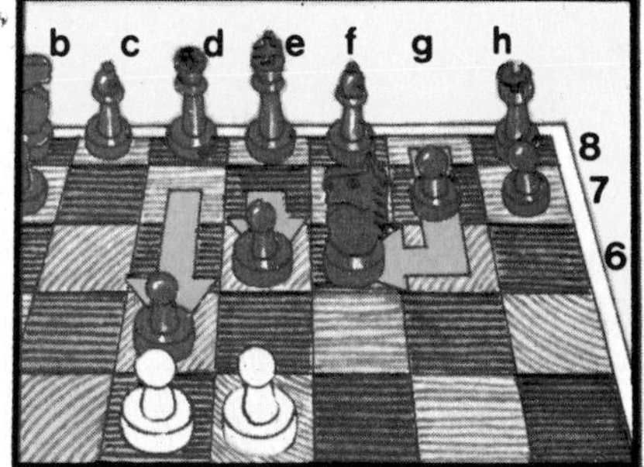

If White's first move is Pawn to e4, play Pawn to e6, followed by Pawn to d5, then, if possible, move your Knight to f6, move the Bishop and then castle.

English opening

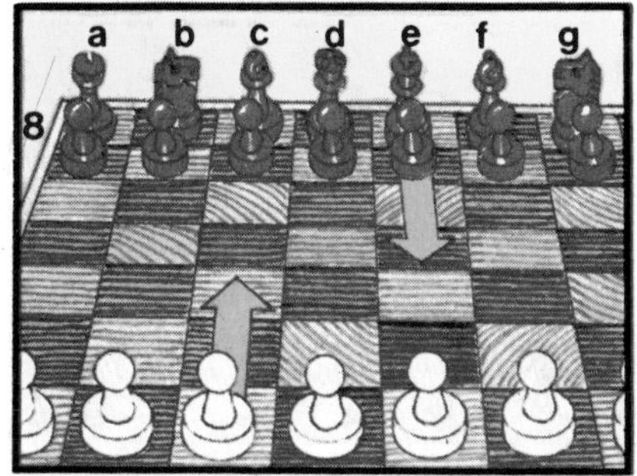

If White opens with 1. c4, reply by moving a Pawn to e5. Both sides are trying to control the center square d5.

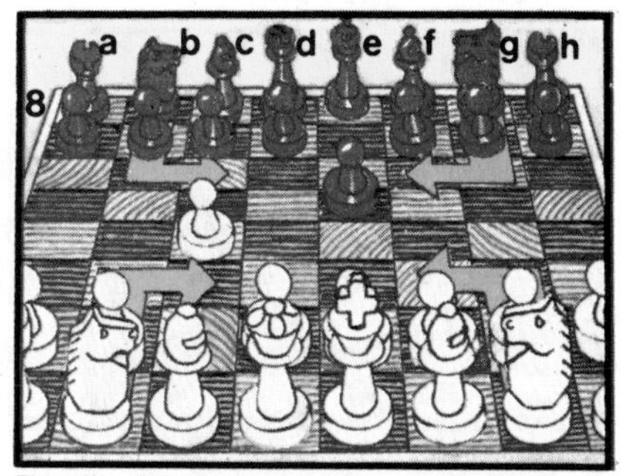

Both sides can bring out their Knights and develop quickly. Black can then move the Bishop to b4, attacking the White Knight.

Reti's opening

If White plays 1. Nf3, reply with 1 . . . d5. If White plays 2. c4, defend your Pawn with 2 . . . e6. White will probably then play Pawn to g3 to open for the Bishop and Black can further defend the Pawn with a Knight on f6.

Both sides can then move their Bishops, and then castle on the King's side.

First moves for White

On these two pages you can follow some more first moves for White. The board on the right shows the positions after both sides have made two moves. For the third move, White should develop a Bishop. The first three pictures below show which square is best for the Bishop.

The rest of the pictures show some of the moves White can make in reply to certain moves from Black.

Both sides have put a Pawn in the center and moved a Knight.

Placing the Bishop

Square d3 is not a good place for the Bishop. It blocks in the Queen's Pawn and is itself shut in by the King's Pawn.

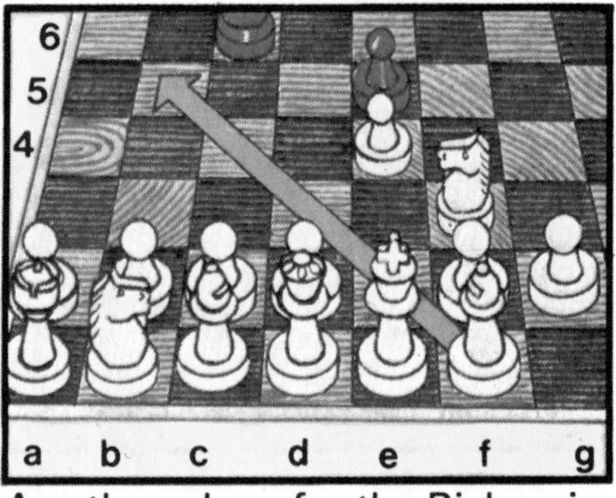

Another place for the Bishop is square b5, but this can lead to complicated positions later in the game.

The best place, here, for the Bishop is c4. It is a good center square from which the Bishop points towards the enemy King.

White's move 4

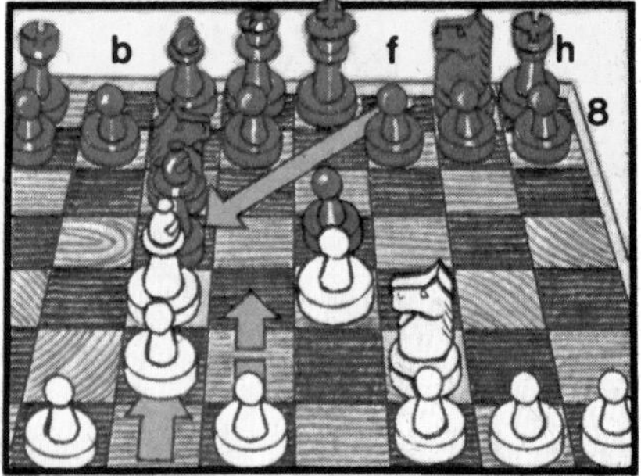

If Black, for his third move, brings out a Bishop, White can put a Pawn on c3, to defend the Pawn he is planning to move to d4 on his next turn.

Choice two for move 4

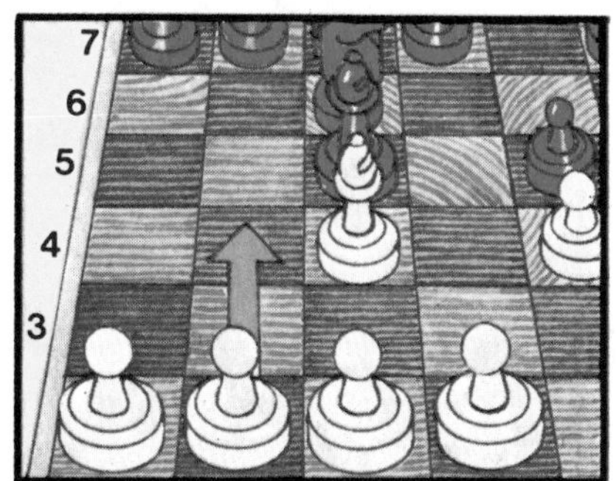

Alternatively, White can put a Pawn on b4, tempting Black to capture it. This is called the "Evan's Gambit".

If Black takes the Pawn, White can move a Pawn to c3, attacking the Bishop to force it to move again.

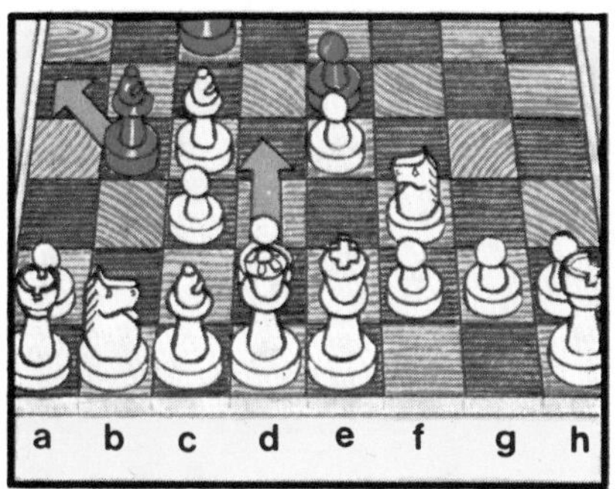

The Bishop moves back and White can move a Pawn to d4, putting another Pawn in the centre and opening for the White Bishop.

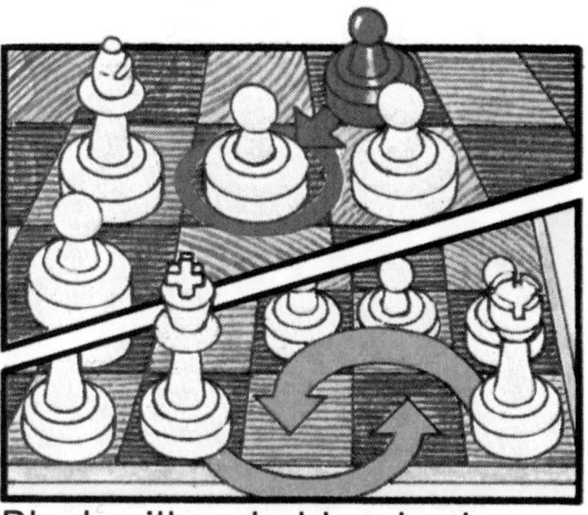

Black will probably take the Pawn, and White can castle. Black was tempted to take two Pawns, and neglect the development of his pieces.

Choice three

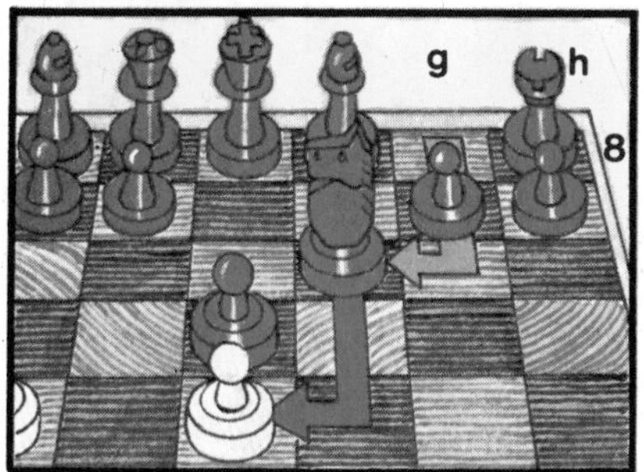

For his third move Black might move a Knight instead of a Bishop. This attacks the Pawn on e4.

If Black does this, White should defend the Pawn with another Pawn on d3, then go on to castle and develop other pieces.

First moves for Black

Black always plays second, so when you play Black, you will be replying to moves that White has made.

On the board on the right, White has placed a Pawn on c4 and is challenging Black to capture it. This is called the "Queen's Gambit".

The pictures on these two pages show what happens if Black takes the Pawn, and what happens if he leaves it.

The board shows the positions after White's second turn.

Black takes the Pawn

If, on move two, Black captures the White Pawn, White will probably bring out the Knight to defend the other Pawn.

White would then move the King's Pawn so the Bishop could take Black's Pawn. White's pieces would then be well placed and ready to castle.

Black leaves the Pawn

Instead of taking the Pawn, Black, for his second move, can bring out another Pawn to e6, protecting the first Pawn.

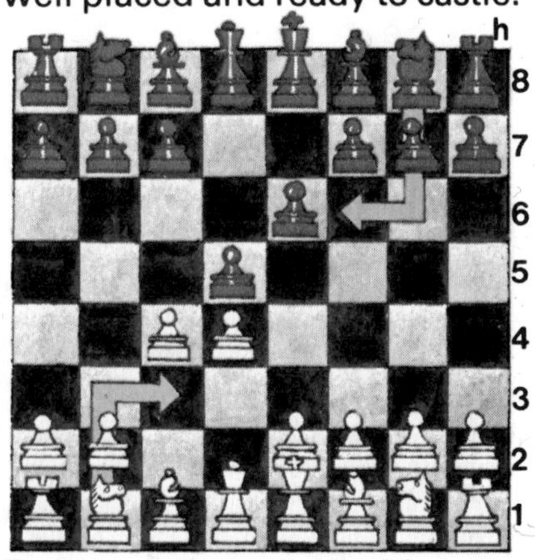

For move three, both sides can bring out Knights.

White, on move four, attacks the Black Knight with a Bishop. Black moves a Bishop to defend the Knight, and is now ready to castle.

White moves a Pawn to open the way for his other Bishop and Black castles. Black's pieces are now well placed.

Third alternative

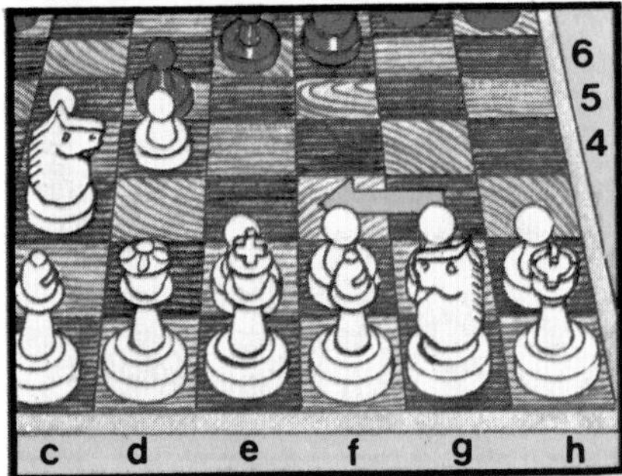

White could have moved a Knight instead of the Bishop on move four. This would defend the Pawn on d4.

Black could then move the Bishop to attack the White Knight on c3, then castle and bring out the other pieces.

Famous chess players

Alexander Alekhine was born in Moscow in 1892. He learned to play chess when he was very young and developed his brilliant game through hard work and practice.

In 1927, Alekhine won the World Championship from the Cuban champion, José Capablanca, who until then had seemed unbeatable. Alekhine lost the title to Max Euwe from Holland in 1935, but regained it in a match two years later and held it until he died in 1946.

The middle game

Now that you have brought out most of your pieces, you should start thinking of ways to win the game, that is, to checkmate the enemy King. You should be planning an attack on your opponent's King and trying to capture enemy pieces to weaken his defenses. On the next few pages there are some special tricks to help you capture pieces. Here, there are general guidelines to help you in this part of the game.

Before you make any move, ask yourself the questions set out below. Make sure you have a reason for each of your moves and try and work out what your opponent will do, to make sure your plan works.

Questions to ask before you move

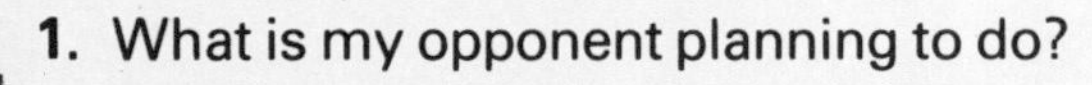

1. What is my opponent planning to do?
2. Are all my pieces defended and are any of them being attacked?

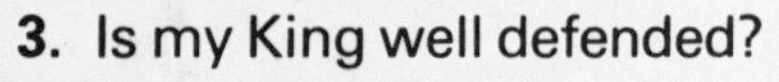

3. Is my King well defended?
4. Can I capture an enemy piece – and is it safe to do so?

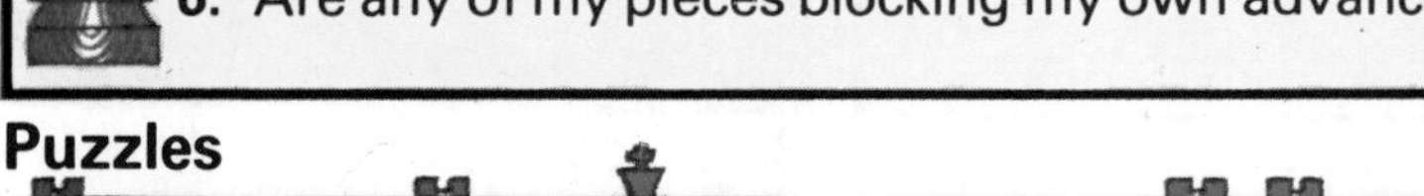

5. Are all my pieces working together as a team?
6. Are any of my pieces blocking my own advance?

Puzzles

On this board, can you see what Black is threatening to do? How can White, who is next to move, prevent it?*

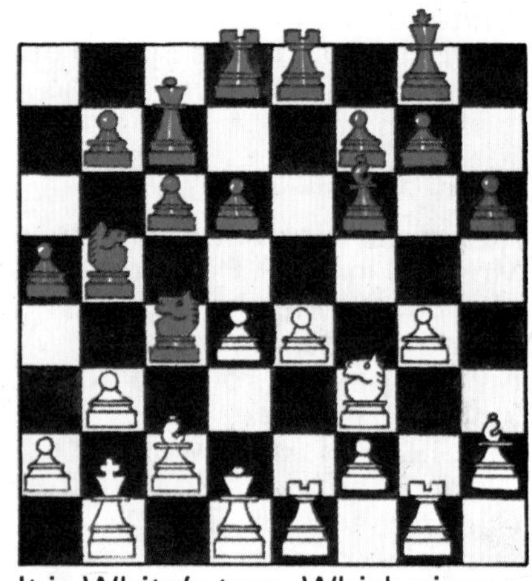

It is White's turn. Which piece can White capture – and is it safe to do so?*

 **Answer page 62*

Points to look out for

Pieces in your way ▶

Some pieces, such as Bishops, are much more powerful on open lines, so be careful not to shut them in with your own pieces. If there is an enemy piece in the way, see if you can force it to move.

On the board on the right, the Black Pawn on d5 is in the White Bishop's way. To make it move, White can take the Black Knight with the White Knight. Black will then capture the White Knight with the Black Pawn, and the line will be open for the Bishop.

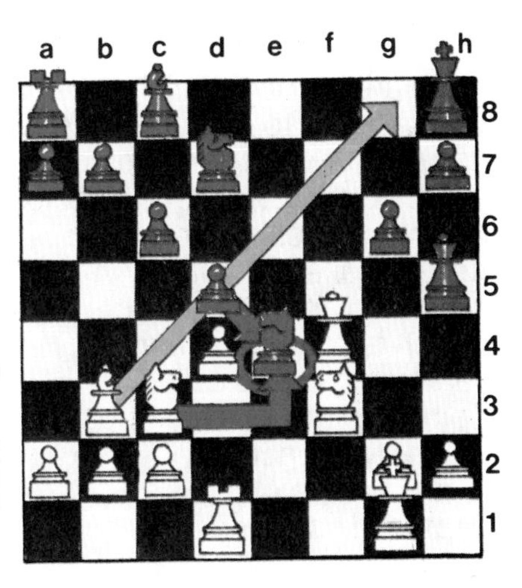

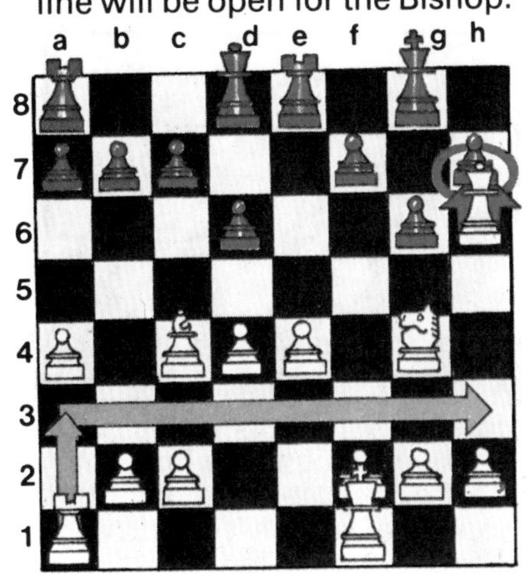

◀ Making your pieces work as a team

An attack on the enemy King is unlikely to work unless you use all your pieces to back each other up.

For example, on the board on the left, the White Rook on a1 is playing no part in the attack on the King. White should move the Rook to a3, then over to h3. From there it can prevent the Black King capturing the Queen after she takes the Pawn on h7. White will then have a strong attack against Black's King.

Powerful Rooks ▶

Two Rooks standing one behind the other or side-by-side, are very powerful as they can defend each other.

On the board on the right, the two White Rooks are especially powerful as they control the whole file. White can move a Rook to e7 to attack Black's Pawns. To defend them, Black must play Rook to c8. White can then move the Rook to d7 and bring the other Rook up to threaten the Black Rook.

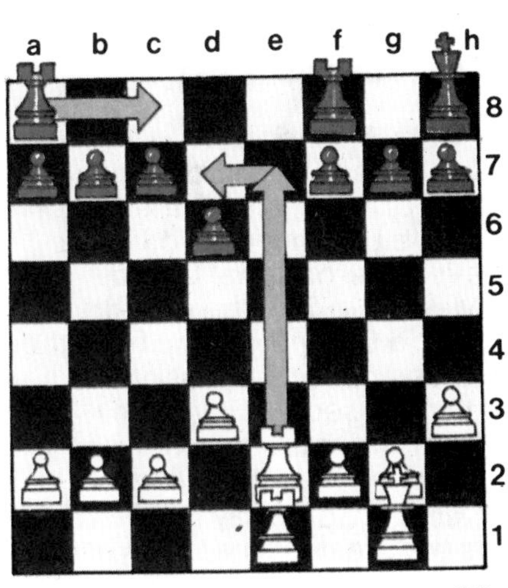

Capturing tricks

Here are some special tricks you can use to capture or tie down your opponent's pieces. An attack by one piece on two enemy pieces at the same time is called a "fork". An attack on an enemy piece which is protecting a more valuable piece is called a "pin". An attack on a valuable piece, forcing it to move so a less valuable piece is captured, is called a "skewer"

Here, the Knight is attacking the Queen and the Rook at the same time. If either of them moves, the other will be captured.

The White Pawn has the Rook and the King in a fork. The King must move out of check, so the Pawn will capture the Rook.

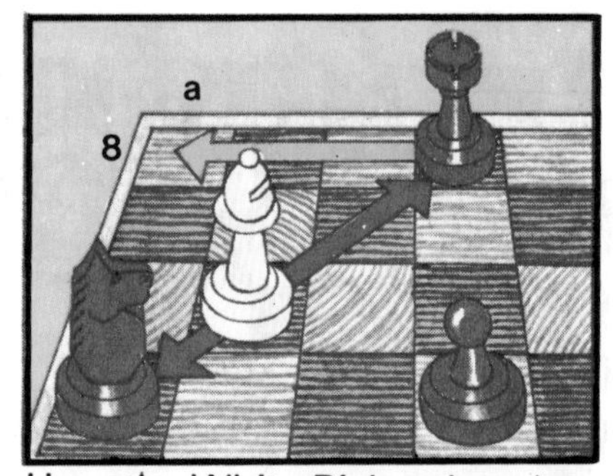

Here the White Bishop has the Rook and Knight in a fork, but Black can escape by moving the Rook to a8 where it can defend the Knight.

Famous chess players

Bobby Fischer, born in 1943, was American Champion when he was only 14, and at the age of 15, he became the youngest ever International Grand Master. In 1972 he won the World Championship from the Russian, Boris Spassky, but he has refused to play in any tournaments since then and forfeited his title to Anatoly Karpov. Some say that Fischer is the greatest chess player ever.

Here, the White Rook is attacking the Black Bishop. The Bishop cannot move, or the Rook will capture the Queen. The Bishop is "pinned" to the Queen.

The Black Knight is pinned to the King by the attack by the White Bishop. The Knight cannot move or the King will be in check.

White can escape from this pin on the Knight by moving the Queen to another square from which it can still protect the Knight.

Here the Queen is being attacked by the Bishop. The Queen has to move and the Bishop will capture the Rook, a less valuable piece.

Chess machine

In 1770, an American called Wolfgang Kempelen, invented a chess machine that could beat nearly anybody who challenged it.

The "machine" was called the Turk and was built in the shape of a man, sitting at a cabinet inside which there were many wires and pulleys. The Turk beat many famous people, including Napoleon, who was not a very good chess player.

At the time, no one knew how the Turk worked, but there must have been a human chess player operating it from inside the cabinet.

Another trick

Another useful trick is called the "discovered attack". This is when you move a piece to open the way for another of your pieces to attack an enemy piece. Watch out for discovered attacks on your own pieces.

Here, the White Bishop is in position to attack the King when the White Pawn moves. This is a discovered attack which will also be check.

On this board, if White moves the Knight to attack the Rook he will reveal a discovered attack by the White Queen on the Bishop.

Here, when the Bishop moves to attack the King, the Rook can attack the Queen. The King must move out of check so White will take the Queen.

Unusual chess games

Scotch chess

In this game, White has one move, then Black has two, White has three and so on. If a player puts the other in check, his turn ends. You have to be very careful in this game, and think far ahead.

Suicide chess

The object of this game is to lose all your pieces, and the player who loses them all first, wins. If a piece can capture another, it must do so, and Kings can be captured like the other pieces.

Capturing puzzles

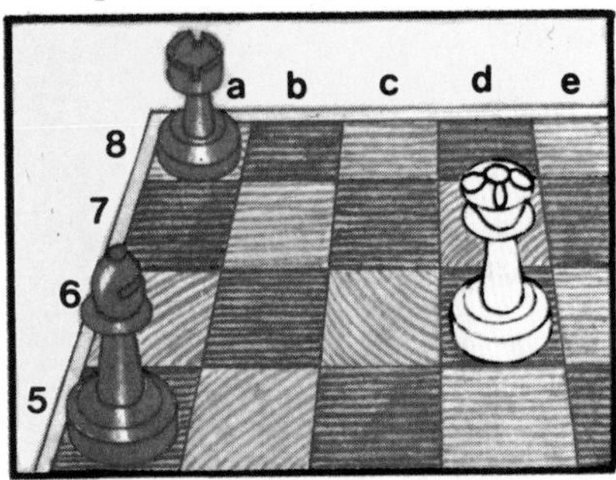

1. Which square can the Queen move to in order to fork the Rook and the Bishop and be safe from attack itself?*

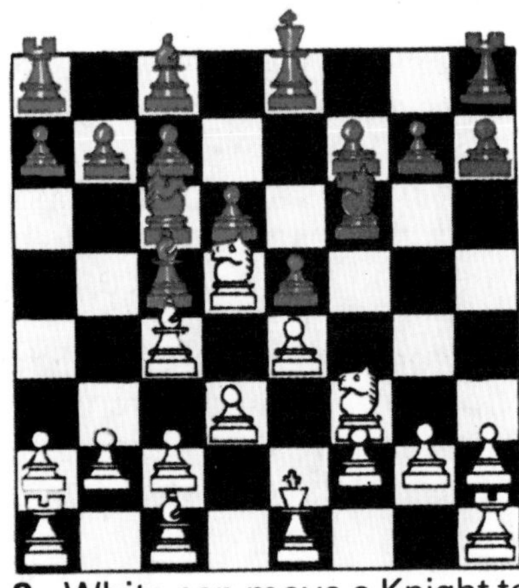

2. White can move a Knight to fork Black and win pieces. How?*

3. The Black Rook is attacking White's Bishop, but White can reply with a pin that wins a piece. How?*

4. Can you find a move for White that is check, and which also wins the Black Queen with a skewer?*

5. White can make a discovered attack on the King.How?*

6. Black has a discovered check that is checkmate. How?*

*Answers page 62

Planning moves

Planning moves in advance is very difficult, as usually you do not know what moves your opponent is going to make. Even Grand Masters do not often think more than two, or perhaps three moves ahead. If, though, you can play several moves that force your opponent to move in a certain way, such as when you attack a piece, or put the King in check, it is much easier to plan ahead.

A series of moves which force certain replies from your opponent is called a combination. In the following example, Black's moves are all forced by White, and the combination of moves leads to checkmate.

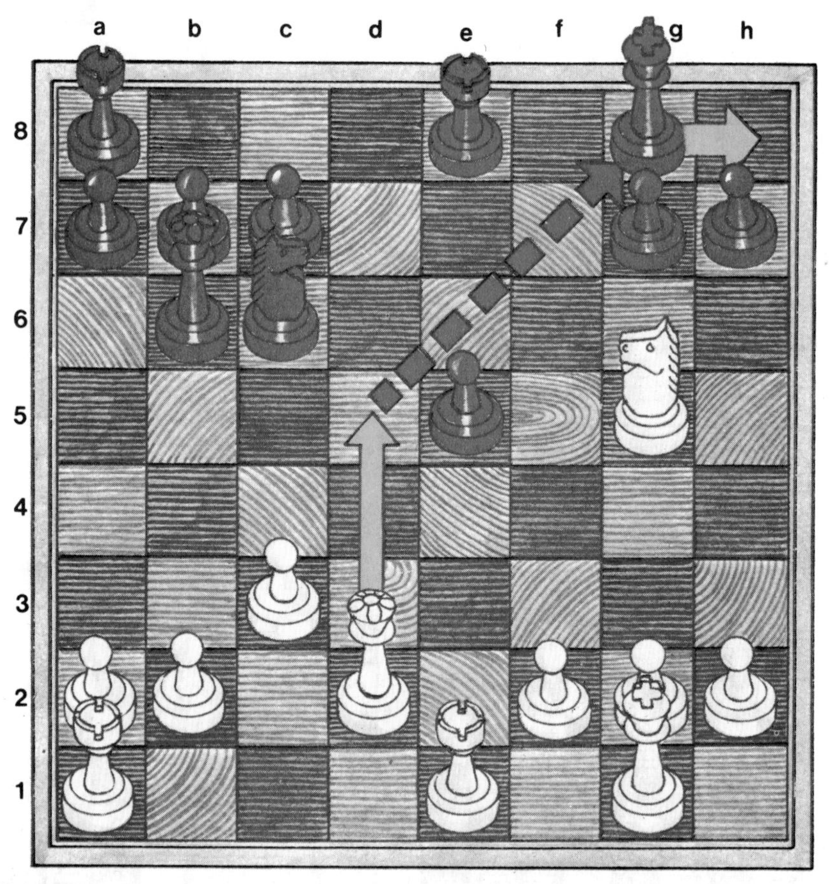

This is the position of the pieces. Both sides have developed their pieces, castled and brought the Queen out to attack.

Now the White Queen moves to d5 and puts the King in check. The Black King cannot move to f8, as the Queen could give checkmate from f7, so his move to h8 is forced.

White then moves the Knight to f7 and puts the King in check again. The King has to move back to g8.

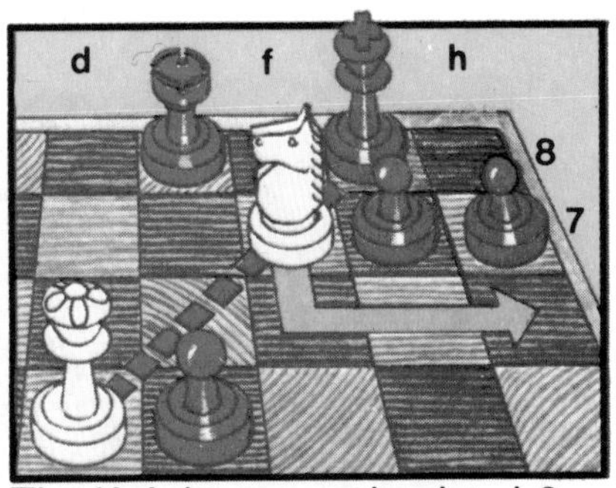

The Knight moves back to h6 and gives check again, and also opens the way for a discovered check from the Queen. This is called double check.

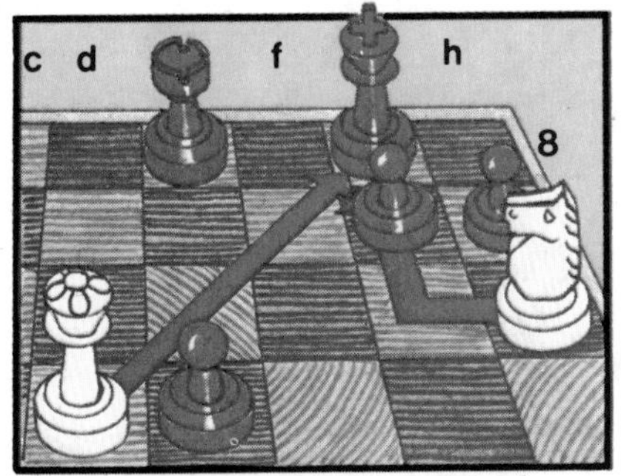

The King must move out of check. Black cannot take the Knight with the Pawn, as the King would still be in check from the Queen.

So the King has to move back to h8 again. He cannot move to f8 as the Queen can still checkmate from f7.

Now the Queen moves to g8 and the King is again in check. It cannot take the Queen, as it would be in check from the Knight.

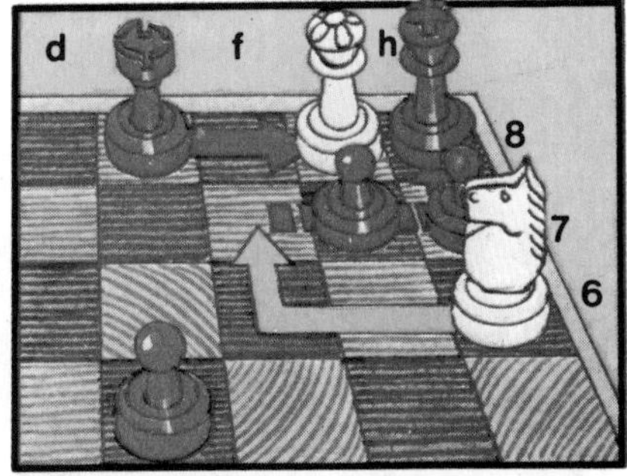

Black has to take the Queen with the Rook. Then the White Knight checkmates the King which is trapped in by its own pieces.

More planned moves

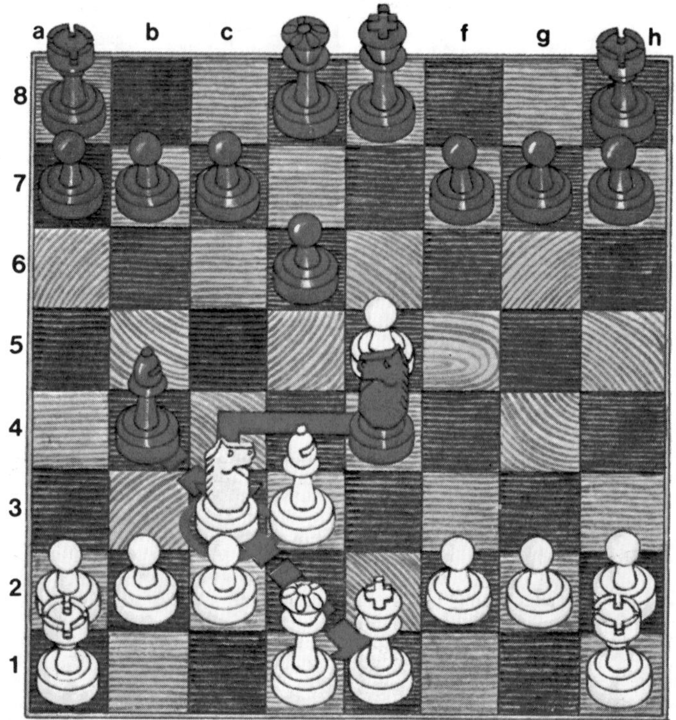

On this board, Black can make some moves which force White's replies and enable Black to fork the White King and Rook. Black's Knight and Bishop are attacking the White Knight which cannot move as it is protecting the White King from the Bishop. Black now captures the White Knight with the Black Knight.

White captures the Black Knight with a Pawn. Both sides have now lost a piece of the same value.

Black takes the Pawn with the Bishop and forks the White Rook and King. The King has to move and Black takes the Rook.

Checkmate combination

These moves are from a game played by Alekhine against an American Grand Master, Reshevsky, in 1937. Alekhine is White and it is his turn to move. The White King is being attacked by the Black Queen and Rook. White, though, can give checkmate first.

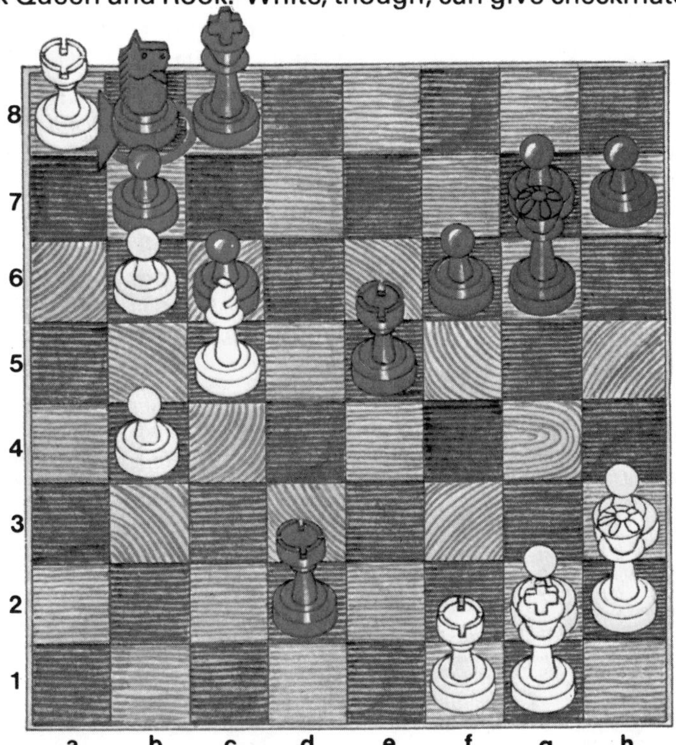

White captures the Knight and puts the Black King in check. Now Black cannot continue his attack as he must move his King out of check.

Black moves out of check by taking the White Rook with the King. White captures the Rook on e5 with the Queen and puts the King in check again.

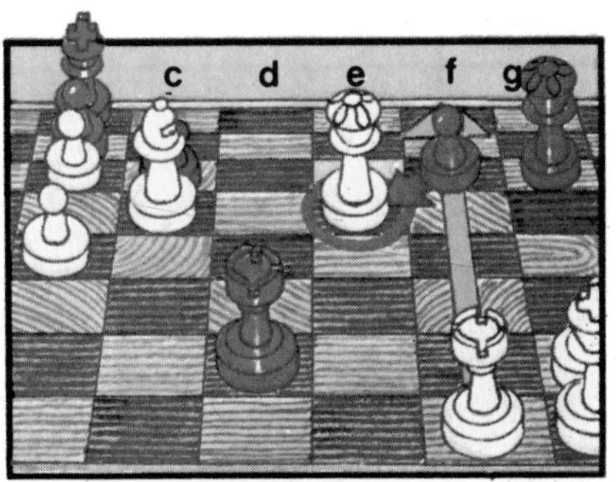

Black takes the Queen and White gives check with the Rook on f8. Black can defend with the Queen and Rook, but White will soon take these and give checkmate.

The endgame

If neither player manages to give checkmate in the middle game, both sides gradually lose most of their pieces. Then they have to try and checkmate their opponent with only a King and one or two other pieces. This stage is called the "endgame". With some combinations of pieces, though, it is not possible to give checkmate, even if your opponent has only a King, and the game will probably end in a draw (see page 20). The chart at the bottom of the page shows which combinations of pieces can force checkmate and which cannot. Here are some points to remember in the endgame.

If you have any Pawns left you should concentrate on getting one of them to the other side of the board so you can make it a Queen (see page 10). For guidelines on how to do this, see pages 50–51.

Try and keep all your pieces on open lines near the center of the board where they are most powerful. Now that you have very few pieces left, you must make sure they are all taking part in the game.

Now is the time to bring out your King and use it as an attacking piece. Your other pieces will need its support and now that there are fewer pieces on the board, it is safer for the King. Guard it carefully though.

Pieces which can give checkmate

These are the combinations of pieces which can and cannot give checkmate against a lone King, or a King and a couple of other pieces, if there are no Pawns on the board.

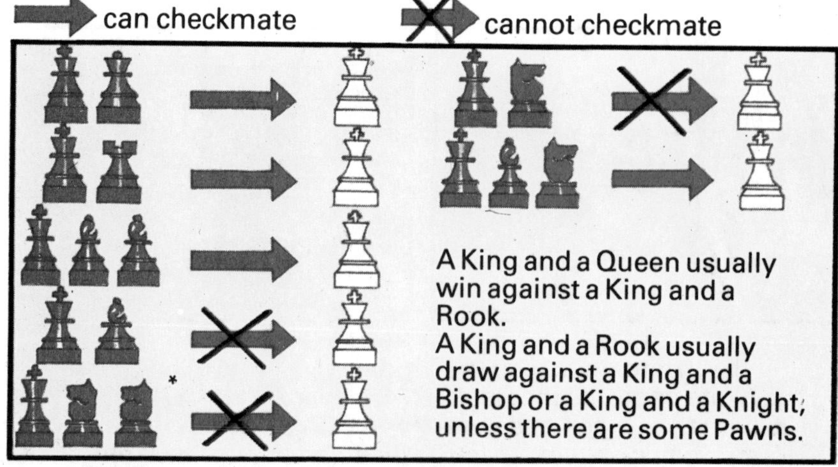

**Checkmate is possible in this situation if the King is in a corner position*

Pawns in the endgame

If, at this stage of the game, you have any Pawns left, they are very valuable, as one of them could become a Queen. If you do manage to Queen a Pawn, you will have a big advantage over your opponent, so move your Pawns very carefully.

Try and avoid having two Pawns behind each other, like Black's Pawns on c-file, as they cannot protect each other. The Black Pawn on the e-file is also weak as it is by itself.

Here, the White g-Pawn is by itself, but is very useful. The Black King has to go to stop it Queening and the White King can capture Black's Pawns.

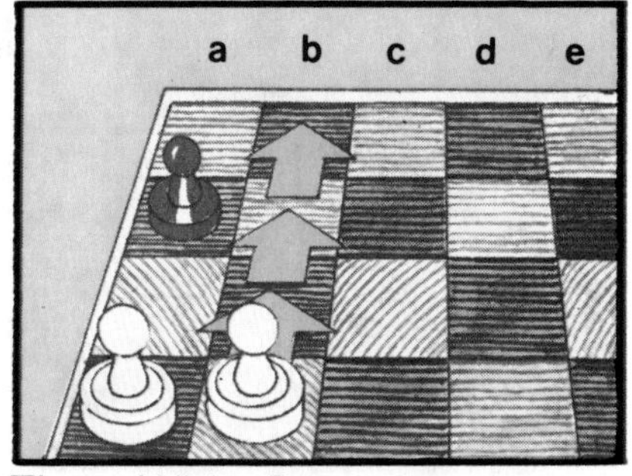

These White Pawns are very strong. The Black Pawn may capture one of them, but there will be no pieces to stop the other becoming a Queen.

You should use your other pieces to help your Pawn become a Queen. Above, the White King is defending all

the squares needed by the White Pawn to reach the other side. A Pawn about to Queen is a very important piece.

Queening a Pawn

To get the White Pawn safely to the other side, White must use the King to defend it. White moves the King to c5, and the Black King moves to b7.

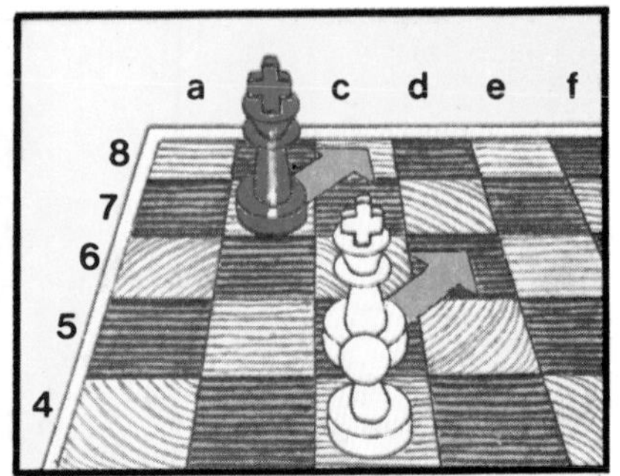

White then moves the King up to d6, and Black tries to cover the Queening square (square where the Pawn will become a Queen).

White moves the Pawn to c5 and Black, with no other pieces, has to move the King. The White King goes to d7 and defends the Pawn until it Queens.

Be careful of this position – with Black to move it is stalemate (see page 20). If White goes first, the King can defend the Queening square. How?*

If the enemy King is far enough away, the Pawn can become a Queen without the help of its King. Imagine a square with the Pawn in one corner. If the enemy King can get into the square, it can catch the Pawn as it reaches the Queening square.

**Answer page 62*

Checkmate in the endgame

If you have Pawns to back up your other pieces in the endgame, it is much easier to checkmate the enemy King. Even if you do lose all your Pawns, you can still give checkmate, though, as shown by the chart on page 48. On the next three pages there are some examples of checkmates with no Pawns.

If you have any Pawns left, you should concentrate on making one of them a Queen. If you have a Bishop left, keep any Pawns you may have on squares of the opposite color to the one the Bishop is standing on, so they do not block it in. If your opponent has a Bishop, your pieces will be safe from attack if they are on squares of the opposite color to the Bishop's.

Checkmate positions

In both these pictures, White has the Black King in checkmate. In both cases the Black King is at the edge of the Board. If you try out some more positions, you will find it is always necessary to force the King to the edge in order to checkmate.

Above, the White King and Queen work together and close in on the King to reduce the number of squares it can escape to. Here are the moves: 1. Ke5, Kc6. 2. Qb4, Kc7. 3. Qb5, Kd8. 4. Qb7, Ke8. 5. Ke6, Kd8. 6. Qd7, checkmate.

More checkmates

On these two pages there are some examples of checkmate by White in endgames where neither side has any Pawns and Black has only a King. It is a good idea to play the moves on a chess set so you learn how to cope with similar situations in your own endgames.

In all the checkmates, White's pieces have to work together to close in on the King and force it to the side.

King and Rook against King

To force the Black King back, White moves the Rook to h6, putting the King in check. Black moves the King to d7.

The white King moves to e5 and the Black King moves away to c7.

White moves the King to d5, chasing the Black King which moves to d7.

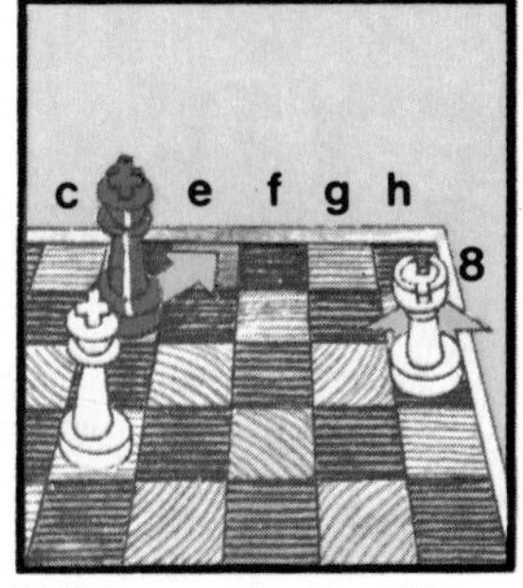

White puts the King in check by moving the Rook to h7. Black moves to e8.

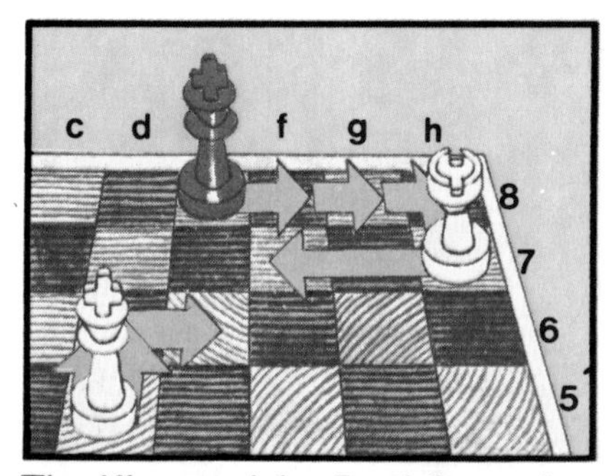

The King and the Rook force the Black King into the corner with the following moves: 5. Kd6, Kf8. 6. Ke6, Kg8. 7. Rf7, Kh8.

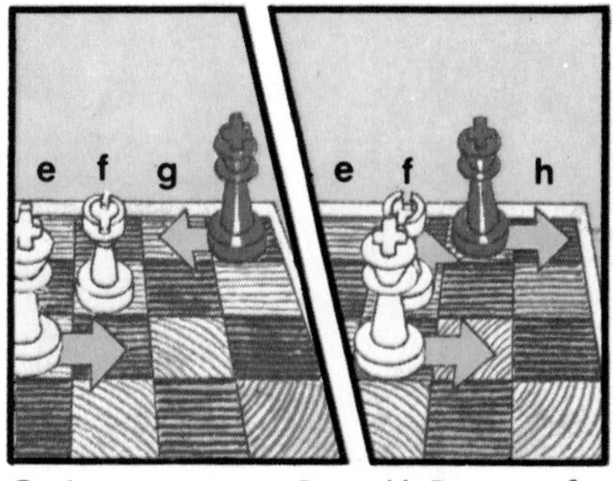

Only squares g8 and h8 are safe for the King now. White gives checkmate with: 8. Kf6, Kg8. 9. Kg6, Kh8. 10. Rf8 checkmate.

King and two Bishops against a King

From the positions shown above, it takes White 12 moves to checkmate. Try the moves on your board and see how the King and both the Bishops work together to force the White King to the corner. Here are the moves: 1. Bd4, Ke7. 2. Bd5, Kf8. 3. Kd6, Ke8. 4. Bg7, Kd8. 5. Bf7, Kc8. 6. Kc6, Kb8. 7. Bc4, Kc8. 8. Bf6, Kb8. 9. Kb6, Kc8. 10. Be6 check, Kb8. 11. Be5 check, Ka8. 12. Bd5 checkmate.

King, Bishop and Knight against King

White moves the Bishop to c8 and Black takes the King to b8, avoiding the corner and square b7 which is attacked by the Bishop.

White moves the Knight to b4, where it will be in a good position at the end of the game. Black moves the King back to a7.

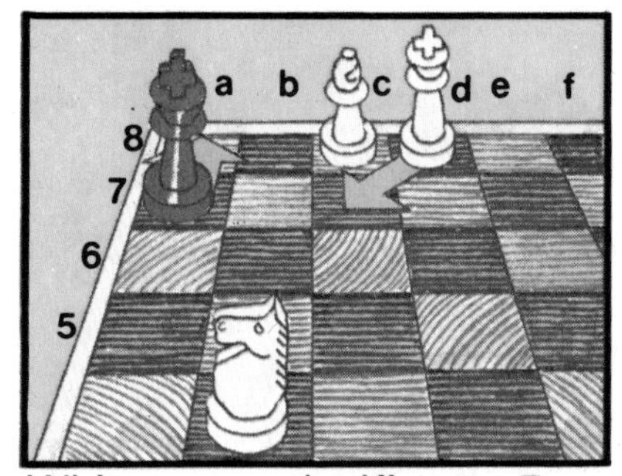

White moves the King to c7, bringing it into the attack. Black is forced to move the King to a8 – the only safe square.

White checks with the Bishop, forcing the King back to a7. White gives checkmate next move. Can you work out how?*

**Answer page 62*

Another game to follow

On the next few pages there is a game played in 1974 by Anatoly Karpov against Victor Korchnoi.

For practice, you could follow this game on your chess set, and try and work out why the players made each of their moves. This is a very good way of improving your chess. Karpov played White.

Karpov was World Chess Champion for ten years. He became Champion in 1975, when Bobby Fischer refused to defend the title.

The opening

The picture below shows the board after the first nine moves, which are listed on the left. The opening was a variation of the Sicilian defense (see page 32).

1. e4, c5
2. Nf3, d6
3. d4, cxd4
4. Nxd4, Nf6
5. Nc3, g6
6. Be3, Bg7
7. f3, Nc6
8. Qd2, 0-0
9. Bc4, Bd7

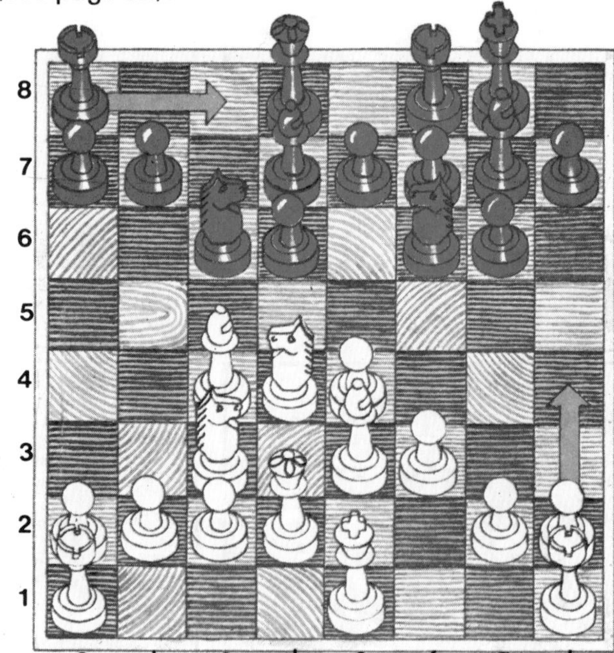

So far, both sides have been developing their pieces. For his tenth move, Karpov starts an attack on Black's King by moving a Pawn to h4. Black replies by moving a Rook along the back rank to c8, preparing for an attack on White's Queen's side.

Positions after 13th move

The game continues with ▶ 11. Bb3, Ne5. White moves a Bishop back and Black opens the file for the Rook. 12. 0-0-0, Nc4. 13. Bxc4, Rxc4. both sides exchange pieces of equal value. The positions of the pieces now are shown on the board on the right. 14. h5, Nxh5. White sacrifices the Pawn on h5, but Karpov hopes that by drawing out the Knight and opening the h-file, he will win a quick victory.

Move 17

◀ White plays 15. g4, bringing another Pawn forward. Black moves the Knight back with 15 . . . Nf6. 16. White moves the Knight on d4 to e2. Black moves the Queen to a5, building up the attack on White's Queen's side. 17. Bh6, Bxh6. White tempts Black to take the Bishop in order to draw the Black Bishop away from the King's defense. The White Queen was defending the Bishop and is now attacking the Black Bishop.

Move 18

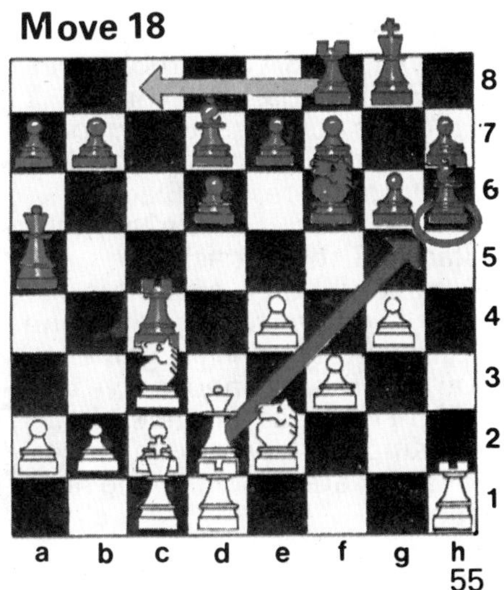

18. Qxh6, R(f8)c8. The White ▶ Queen takes the Bishop and Black moves the Rook on f8 to attack White's Queen's side.

The positions are now as shown by the arrows on the board on the right. White's attack on the Black King is very strong, with both the Queen and the Rook bearing down the open file towards the King. Korchnoi is trying to organize an attack on the other side of the board, but he has miscalculated the strength of White's attack.

Moves 19 and 20

The next moves are shown on the board on the right. 19. Rd3, R(c4)c5. (The letters in brackets show which Rook moved.)

Black was hoping to capture the White Knight on c3, so Karpov moved the White Rook to defend it. Korchnoi replied by moving his Rook back a square. 20. g5, Rxg5. Karpov sacrifices another Pawn, but his next move puts his opponent in a very difficult position.

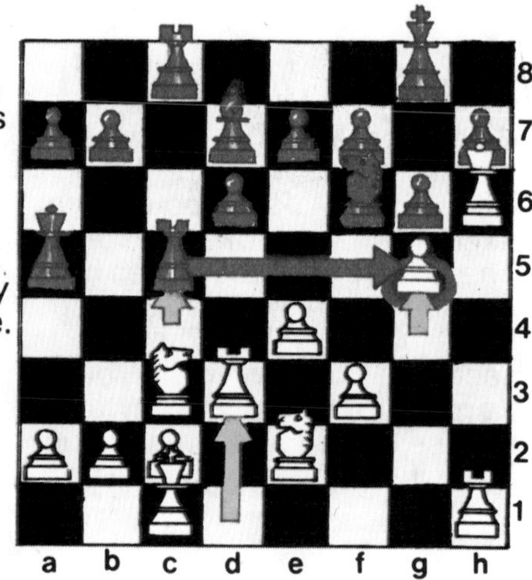

Move 21

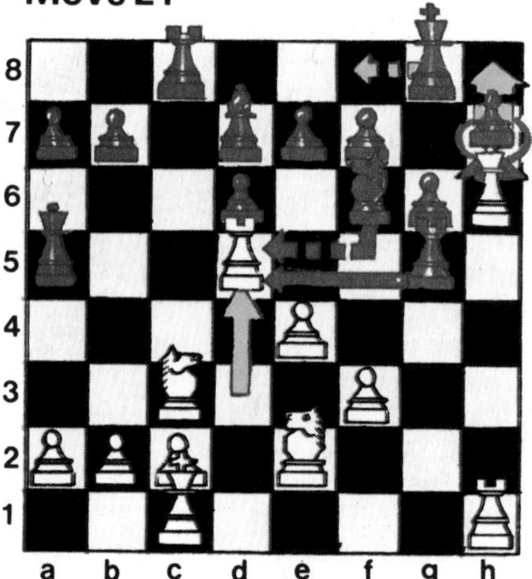

White plays 21. Rd5. Now, if Black plays 21. Nxd5, capturing the Rook with the Knight, he will leave his King undefended. White would then checkmate with 22. Qxh7, Kf8 and 23. Qh8 checkmate. These moves are shown with dotted arrows on the board on the left.

If Black does not take the Rook at all, he will lose his Rook on g5. So Korchnoi is forced to play 21. Rxd5, capturing White's Rook.

Moves 22 to 24

22. Nxd5, Re8. White recaptures the Rook on d5. The White Knight is now threatening to capture the Black Pawn on e7 and from there, fork Black's King and Rook. 23. N(e2)f4, Bc6. Black's Bishop attacks the White Knight. 24. e5. This is a very strong move for White and will eventually win the game for Karpov. Black cannot move the Knight on f6, as it is defending the King. Other possible moves for Black are shown on the next page.

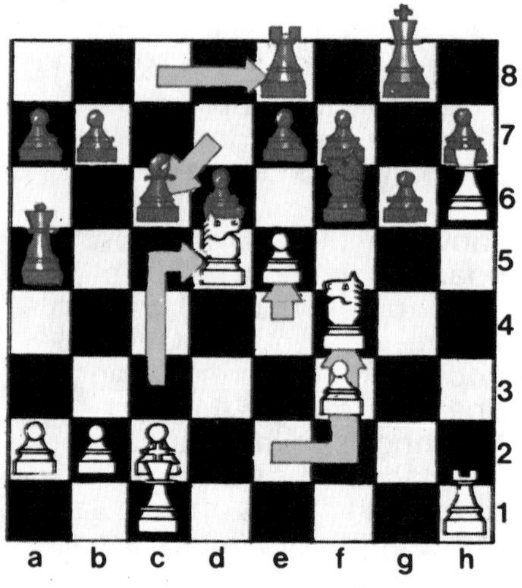

Possible moves for Black for move 24

Black could capture the Pawn on e5 with 24 . . . dxe5. White would then win, though, in the next four moves.

25. Nxf6 check. White could take the Black Knight defending the King, putting the King in check.

The Black Pawn could capture the Knight with 25 . . . exf6, and White could play 26. Nh5, threatening checkmate with the Queen on g7.

If Black plays 26 . . . gxh5, taking the Knight with the Pawn, this leaves the g-file open and White can play 27. Rg1 check.

Black has to move the King out of check with 27 . . . Kh8, and White then checkmates with 28. Qh7. Korchnoi decided to play 24 . . . Bxd5, capturing the Knight.

Black's move 24

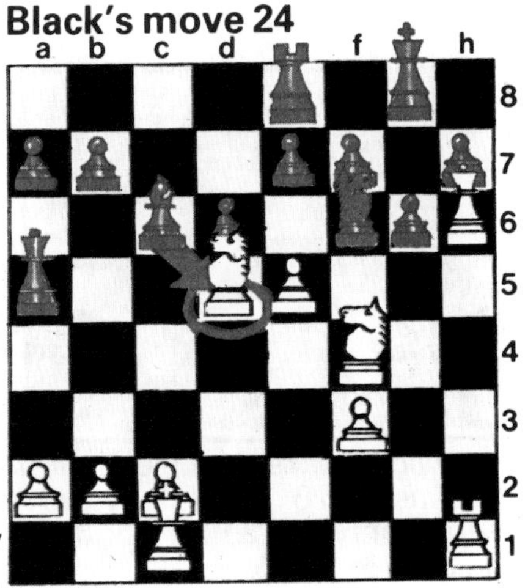

The end of the game

White plays 25. exf6, capturing the Knight defending Black's King. Black recaptures White's Pawn with 25 . . . exf6.

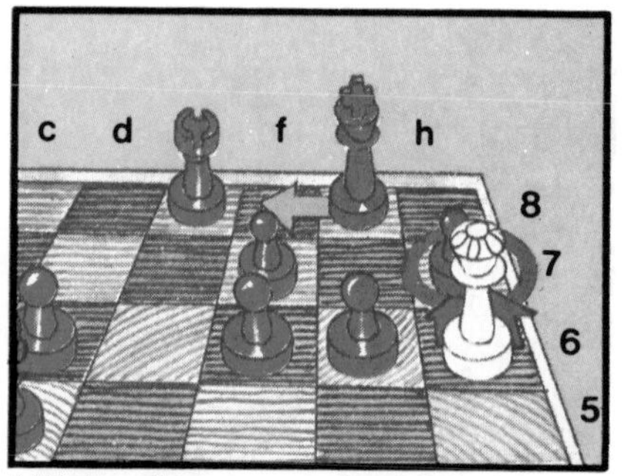

White then puts the King in check with 26. Qxh7, taking the Pawn with the Queen. Black moves the King to f8 with 26 . . . Kf8.

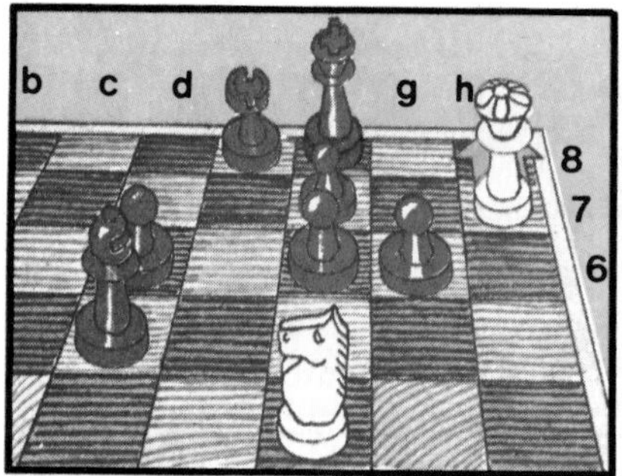

White chases the King with 27. Qh8 and Korchnoi resigns, knowing he cannot avoid defeat, as shown in the next few pictures.

For move 27 Korchnoi would be forced to move the King to e7. White would then play 28. Nxd5 check.

Black could take the Knight with the Queen: 28 . . . Qxd5. White would then play 29. Re1, putting the King in check again.

Wherever the King moves, White could capture the Rook and then win with a King, Queen and Rook against Black's King and Queen.

Another way to write chess moves

Some books and newspapers use a system of writing down moves called descriptive notation, so it is a good idea to be able to read this, as well as algebraic notation explained on page 21.

Each of the pieces is called by its first letter, except for the Knight which is called N or Kt, as shown above.

The pieces which start on the Queen's side are called the Queen's pieces, and those on the King's side are the King's.

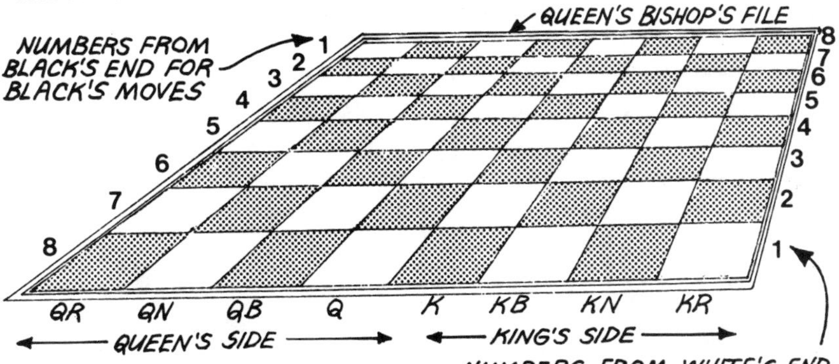

Each file is called by the name of the piece which starts there, and the ranks are numbered.

For White's moves the ranks are numbered from White's end and for Black's, from Black's end.

Examples

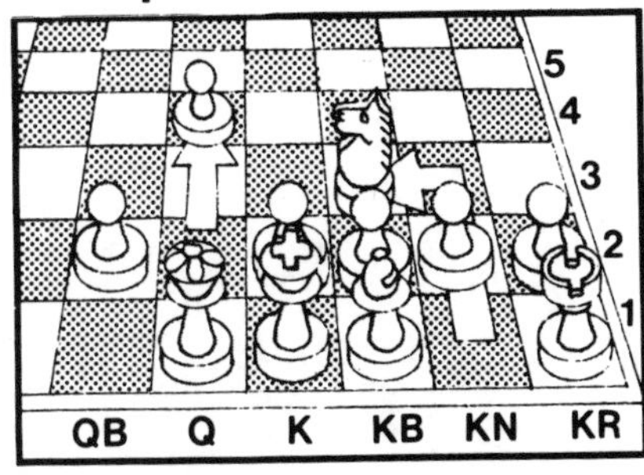

This Knight's move is written N-KB3, in other words, Knight to King's Bishop's file, square three. The Pawn's move is P-Q4. Castling is 0-0 on King's side and 0-0-0 on Queen's side.

These moves for Black are B-Q2 for the Bishop and P-K4 for the Pawn. Capture is shown by "x" between the names of the pieces.

Puzzle answers

The White Bishop can capture only the Black Knight.

The White Rook can take the Black Bishop or the Black Pawn.

The White Rook can capture the Knight, but not the Pawn as the Black Rook would recapture it.

The Black Queen can capture the White Pawn or the White Knight. The White Queen can capture only the Black Knight.

The Bishop should take the Black Rook. It will be recaptured, but White loses a piece worth 3 points, and Black, 5 points.

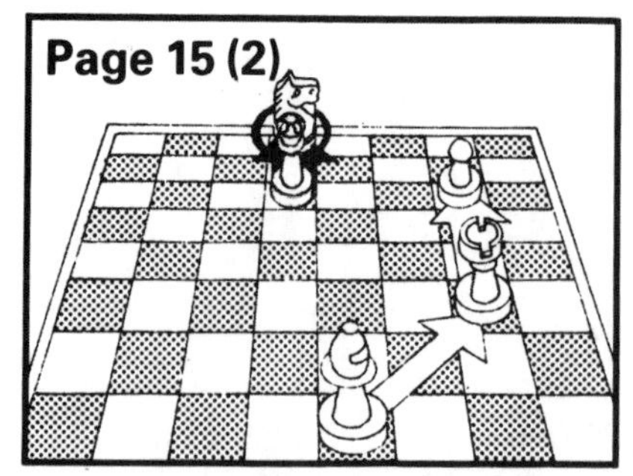

The Black Queen can take the Knight, but not the Pawn which is protected by the Rook, or the Rook protected by the Bishop.

The White Knight should take the Black Bishop. It will be recaptured by the Black Rook, but it will be a fair exchange.

Page 16 (left)

The White Knight cannot safely move to attack the Rook as the square is guarded by the Bishop.

Page 16 (right)

The Bishop is not defended. The Knight is defended by the Rook, and the Rook, by the Pawn.

Page 18

On the left-hand board, both Black and White can castle only on the King's side. On White's Queen's side the Rook has already moved, and on Black's, the Bishop is in the way.

On the right-hand board, White can castle on the King's side but not on the Queen's as the King would pass over a square guarded by the Black Bishop, and this is not allowed. Black can castle on the Queen's side, but not on the King's as the square the King would move to is guarded by the White Bishop.

Page 19 *En passant*

Black can capture *en passant* in pictures 1 and 2, and in the normal way in picture 3.

The White Knight can attack the Rook.

The White Queen can move one square to the right to attack the Knight.

Black can move the Knight to defend the Rook, as shown.

White can checkmate by moving the Knight as shown.

This move by the Queen gives checkmate for White.

Page 25 (left)

The White King cannot castle as the Knight is in the way.

Page 31

White can checkmate by moving the Bishop to capture the Pawn on f7. King's escape is guarded by the Rook on d1.

Page 38 (left)

Black is threatening checkmate by moving the Queen to a2, so White must move a Pawn to b3, to stop the Queen's advance.

Page 43 (1)

If the Queen moves to square d5, it can fork the Rook and Bishop, and be safe from attack.

Page 43 (3)

White can move the Bishop to c6 and pin the Rook to the King. Black moves the King and White can take the Rook.

Page 43 (5)

If White moves the Knight to f4 it reveals a discovered attack by the White Bishop on the Black King.

Page 50

The White King can cover the Queening square by the following moves: 1. Kb6, Kd7. 2. Kb7.

Page 25 (right)

Black can move the Pawn to attack the Knight and make it move.

Page 38 (right)

White can capture the Knight on c4 with the Pawn, but it would be a mistake. Black would move the other Knight to c3 and make a fork on the King and Queen.

Page 43 (2)

White can move the Knight to c7, capturing the Pawn and forking the Rook and King. The King must move out of check and White can take the Rook.

Page 43 (4)

White can move the Rook to h8, making a skewer on the King and Queen. The King must move and White takes the Queen.

Page 43 (6)

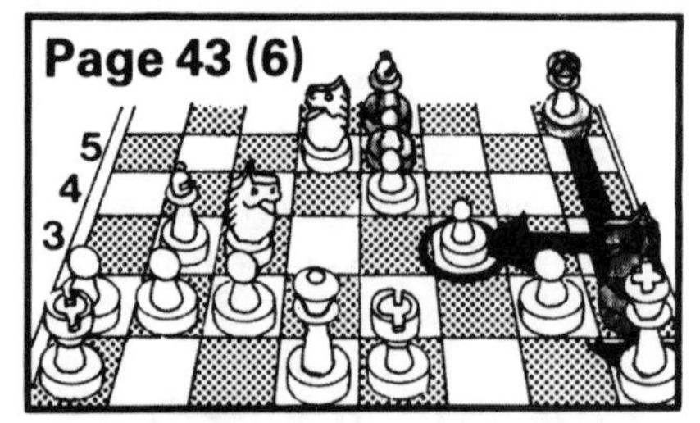

Black moves the Knight to f3 and reveals a discovered check on the King by the Queen. Escape square g1 is covered by the Black Knight.

Page 53

White moves the Knight to c6. All the King's escape squares are covered.

Going further

The best way to improve your chess is to play as often as possible. If you play against someone slightly better than you, this will really improve your game, as you can learn from watching their moves. Do not be put off if you lose a lot of games at first, as you will probably learn from your mistakes. If you join a chess club, you will get a lot of practice playing against different people. There will probably be a club at your school, or you can ask for details of clubs at your local library.

Another way to practice and improve your game is to read books on chess and follow the games printed in chess magazines. When you follow the games of great players, try and work out why they made each of their moves, and what their next move will be.

Chess organizations

The following organizations will give you information about chess events, tournaments and local clubs.

American Chess Foundation
353 West 46th Street
New York, NY 10036
Tel: 1-212-757-0613

The Chess Federation of Canada
Box 7339
Ottawa
Ontario K1L8E4
Canada
Tel: 1-613-733-2844

United States Chess Federation
186 Route 9 West
New Windsor, NY 12553
Tel: 1-800-388-KING

Chess words

Here are some words used in chess, and what they mean. To find out more about any of the words, turn to the page numbers given in brackets with each word.

Castling A special move for the King and the Rook. The King moves two squares to the side of the board and the Rook jumps over the King (page 18).

Developing Moving pieces early in the game to good squares in the center of the board (page 24).

Diagonal A line of squares diagonally across the board (page 5).

Discovered attack An attack by an enemy piece that is only revealed when another enemy piece moves out of the way

Endgame The last part of the game when players have very few pieces left (page 48).

En passant A special rule which allows a Pawn to capture an enemy Pawn which has moved two squares, as though it has moved only one square (page 19).

File A line of squares up and down the board (page 5).

Fork An attack by one piece on two pieces at the same time (page 40).

King's side The side of the board on which the King starts. For White, the right-hand side of the board, and for Black, the left (page 5).

Notation The code for writing down chess moves. One system is called algebraic notation (page 21). Another system is called descriptive notation (page 59).

Perpetual check One player puts the other repeatedly in check and the game ends in a draw (page 20).

Pin An attack on a piece which cannot move, because if it did it would open the way for a more valuable piece to be attacked (page 40).

Queening a Pawn Making a Pawn which has reached the other side of the board, into a Queen (pages 10, 49, 50).

Queen's side The side of the board on which the Queen starts. For White, the left-hand side of the board and for Black, the right-hand side of the board (page 4).

Rank A line of squares across the board (page 5).

Skewer An attack on a valuable piece which, when it moves exposes a less valuable piece to attack and capture (page 40).

Stalemate A game which ends in a draw because one player can make no legal move, but is not in check (page 20).